D0072395

Machiavelli on Management

MACHIAVELLI ON MANAGEMENT

PLAYING AND WINNING THE CORPORATE POWER GAME

Gerald R. Griffin

PRAEGER

New York
Westport, Connecticut
London

Copyright Acknowledgments

The author and publisher are grateful to the following publisher and authors for permission to reprint the Machiavellian Orientation Inventory (appearing here as "The M Factor: Test Your Machiavellian IQ").

Christie, R., and Geis, F. L. *Studies in Machiavellianism*. New York and London: Academic Press, 1970.

Library of Congress Cataloging-in-Publication Data

Griffin, Gerald R., 1944–
    Machiavelli on management : playing and winning the corporate
      power game / Gerald R. Griffin.
      p.   cm.
    Includes bibliographical references (p.) and index.
    ISBN 0-275-93699-6 (alk. paper)
    1. Leadership. 2. Executive ability. 3. Management. 4. Office
politics. 5. Success in business.   I. Title
HD57.7.G75 1991
658.4'095—dc20   90-7804

British Library Cataloguing in Publication Data is available.

Copyright © 1991 by Gerald R. Griffin

All rights reserved. No portion of this book may be
reproduced, by any process or technique, without the
express written consent of the publisher.

Library of Congress Catalog Card Number: 90-7804
ISBN: 0-275-93699-6

First published in 1991

Praeger Publishers, One Madison Avenue, New York, NY 10010
An imprint of Greenwood Publishing Group, Inc.

Printed in the United States of America

∞

The paper used in this book complies with the
Permanent Paper Standard issued by the National
Information Standards Organization (Z39.48–1984).

10 9 8 7 6 5 4 3 2 1

**LIBRARY
ALMA COLLEGE
ALMA, MICHIGAN**

The Will to Power

But you and we should say what we really think, and aim only at what is possible, for we both alike know that into the discussion of human affairs the question of justice only enters where the pressure of necessity is equal, and the powerful exact what they can, and the weak grant what they must.

Athenian declaration at a conference between representatives of Athens and those of Melos in 416 B.C., according to Thucydides

Contents

Preface

> It is customary for those who seek a prince's favor, to present them-
> selves, before him with such things of theirs as they themselves most
> value, . . . I have found among my possessions none that I so much
> prize and esteem as a knowledge of the actions of great men, acquired
> in the course of a long experience of modern affairs and a continual
> study of antiquity.
>
> *The Prince*: vii–viii

These are the words of a man who, for hundreds of years, has been deemed the supreme thinker about survival in the world of politics. Niccolò Machiavelli was able to hit the target with ideas that are as applicable for twentieth-century business organizations as they were for sixteenth-century political organizations. Throughout the centuries he had and has both admirers and detractors. However, a careful analysis of his writings shows that he was the ultimate organizational person. He understood and advised the princes of his day to be goal-setters, to set reachable objectives, and to let nothing stand in their way in achieving those objectives.

He gained this understanding through the study of ancient organizations and of the management styles of princes, kings, and emperors. From this study and analysis of thousands of years of organizational behavior, he gleaned "the true principles of management."

I have taken his ideas and translated them into contemporary management principles that you can utilize on your journey to becoming a successful manager. These are not trite statements for success that are read with ease, but hardly ever work in practice. They are not mere statements about "how things should be." They are the synthesis of "how things are." These ideas are the "management meat" of real managers, of those managers who wish to be extraordinary, and of those managers who wish to be leaders in a dog-eat-dog world.

While Machiavelli was not familiar with corporate takeovers or management reorganization, he certainly would have recognized the characters and characteristics of them. He did not invent new ideas about immoral methods in politics; he looked around and reported what he saw. His thoughts presaged insider trading, corporate hatchetmen, two-faced employees, and corporate sabotage.

The Roman emperors he studied have been replaced by CEOs, the princes by managers with a variety of titles, and the kingdoms and states by organizations of all designs and sizes. Battles for life and death have been replaced by corporate takeovers and reorganization.

What the generals of old did, the managers of today do. The planning, organizing, directing, and controlling at all levels of management are the same activities as the gaining and maintaining of armies, sustaining of certain losses, and conquering the enemy in the name of what the conqueror—the manager—defines as right.

But the essence, the guts of organizational conquest and of success as a leader, remain the same. The elements of leadership necessary to lead the Roman legions are the same elements necessary to lead a department staff, a division, or a multinational corporation. By analyzing and thinking about the thoughts of Machiavelli, you can gain management success in the twilight of the twentieth century that will insure your future in the dawn of the twenty-first century.

The writings of Machiavelli cover thousands of pages of detailed analysis of the concepts of leadership, the keys to management success, the functioning of organizations, and the various styles of management. His ideas give insight into virtually every important management topic. Although his works were banned for hundreds of years and recommended for total destruction during the Inquisition, his ideas are available today for study by modern managers.

Until now the ideas of Machiavelli have been applied to political organizations and to the actions of political leaders. The few attempts to apply his thoughts to businesses have been superficial. After years of reading and thinking about Machiavelli's analysis of ancient organizations, comparing those organizations with contemporary ones, comparing the successes and failures of emperors and generals of the past with the actions of CEOs and managers of today, I am able to offer you a concise guide to the principles of management as filtered through Machiavellian thought.

I am able to show you how to become a successful manager by helping you to understand that power games are played daily in organizations worldwide—including your own. And if you learn and understand these games, you are then able to play them—and win. Indeed, by winning you gain power and are able to put it to use. Not unscrupulous, dirty power that cares only for selfish aims, but compassionate power that is concerned not only with the self, but with the group—the organization.

In your search for power it is important to realize that power is not divided into discrete categories. It is neither unscrupulous nor compassionate. It is only power—raw power. It is in how managers utilize power—through both their words and deeds—that power becomes good or bad, clean or dirty. Power is present within every organization, and what is not gained by you will be gained by another—perhaps a friend, but more likely an opponent. Therefore, if you care that power be used mercifully, it is indisputably your responsibility to gain the maximum amount possible and use it in a responsible manner.

And this can be done only through thoughtful study and then the putting into action of what you learn.

I have labeled the use of Machiavellian ideas in management, Theory M. And I will relate to you how the Theory M manager differs from, and is more successful than, the stereotyped Theory X or Theory Y manager. This book and your study will make your quest for power and search for excellence less difficult.

I have but one goal in this endeavor, and that is to make you a successful manager—a wise manager, a person who uses power compassionately. You may ask, Why? Is a person who advocates the use of power for success a nice person—one who can be listened to? Surely you have heard the old adage, Watch out for those who say, ''I just want to help you.'' Or you may have been brought up to believe that power is evil and that those who acquire and utilize it are evil.

Indeed, I like to think I am a nice person, but that is not the only reason I have this lofty goal of helping you become a success. I look around at world events and see a dangerous situation evolving. As old tensions are lessened, I know, through my study of power, that new ones, imagined only by the few, will be released. Economic might will replace military might. Economic wars will replace many of the military ones, but their consequence will be the same—there will be winners and losers. And these new wars will be fought by a new breed of battlefield generals—the prince and the general of past skirmishes will become the manager and the executive of the new battles. So if these thoughts will assist in making the victors the compassionate managers, the ones who understand and use power with care, the world will become a better place—for me and those

I care about. The logic then follows that it also becomes a better place for you and those you care about.

But let me give you some warnings. Let me establish some ground rules before you begin to read or follow the courses of action presented in this book. While I have stated Machiavelli's thoughts in contemporary terms and have reduced much of the complexity into easily understandable ideas, I have not reduced the ideas to simplistic formulas to be memorized and forgotten. I have not ground the "meat" into mush for managers who are only babies and need pablum for their existence. This book is for leaders and managers who want to be better than average. This book is for those who truly believe they are number one and want to be the best.

I expect this book to be read by everyone who wants to be a success, but I know that only a few, the extraordinary, will become the success they want to be.

With this book you get the *truth* that the successful have tried to hide from you. You get the principles that academics have confused you with. And instead of the false promise of a magic cure to make you successful, you get a reliable road map for your journey to becoming a success.

WARNING 1

This treatise on becoming successful in management neither strives for nor pretends to be a manual for logical deduction. Often the things managers do defy logic. This is as much a manual for organizational survival as it is a text for those who want to be successful managers. Existence in the world of groups, clubs, cliques, and multinational organizations—without this guide—is tantamount to organizational suicide. The risk that you take by attempting to live in an organization without it is not worth the heartache and tears—amid a world of "it and they."

The thoughts are presented in rapid succession and frequently with coarseness of thought. But as beauty lies in the eyes of the beholder, so management decisions are perceived in the eyes of those who manage. Machiavelli spoke in terms that were familiar to leaders of the sixteenth century. His rhetoric was earthy and his ideas were a harbinger of the science of management. War, murder, and calumny were not born in his heart, nor were they liquidated in his time. They are here today and have found their own definition in modern-day corporate life.

Just as Machiavellian thought has stood the test of time, in victory and leadership, so it finds a home in the heart of every manager or would-be manager. The prince Machiavelli sought to please and assist is no different than the corporate president, or frontline supervisor, who seeks success each day. The states, armies and governments of sixteenth-century Italy and France find their analogy in the companies, staffs, and work groups of this century.

While Machiavelli did not write to the queens and princesses of his day, they were certainly as successful (and ruthless) in the management of their organizations as the kings and princes were. And I have written this book for both the woman and the man who would be a "manager-prince."

WARNING 2

When reading this book you must not be too quick to say, "Yes, I know a manager who thinks like that," or "The merger is good for someone else, but not for me." Judgments in the corporate world come too easily, and in organizational life they are most often directed toward "them" and "the others." Be objective in your reading. What you may do—or plan to do—to another person, may happen to you someday. So analyze and study the concepts from many different perspectives.

WARNING 3

This book is not for everyone. It is only for those managers who want to be at the vanguard of their organizations, to set goals and reach them. For those who feel a certain inward feeling (more than job satisfaction) when they define right, truth, and justice, this book is a must. It is for those managers who wish to use legitimate powers effectively without oppressing others.

WARNING 4

In your quest for power, remember that status is an important component of a person's organizational psyche. Before you confront opponents or depend on allies, you need to know what their aspirations and motivations are, what causes them to act. Likewise you need to know who you yourself are and where you are going.

This book will help you determine that. After reading it, you should know your true thoughts about power and be able to put them into action. If you are afraid to know who you are, do not read any further. Pass the book on to a friend who wants to be successful.

WARNING 5

While most managers soft-sell their need for goal achievement with the need to be self-actualized, and justify their individual and corporate greed by encouraging employees to give to charity or by offering employees profit-sharing programs, this book does not soft-sell or justify any actions of managers.

It does not pretend to be moral, nor does it strive to be amoral. It is not a case book about companies in the United States, or Japan, although it describes the activities of every organization and the actions of millions of managers throughout the world. It is not a book about self-fulfillment. But it describes what a manager needs to know in order to reach excellence in his management career. It is a book about the effective use of creative power.

WARNING 6

This is a book that expects you to be smarter than most managers. Some of the ideas are fairly simple, some complex. And as in any self-education endeavor, you get out of it what you put into it. If you do not want to be a thinking manager, you probably should not read this book. However, if you follow the principles, concepts, and ideas presented, you will become more successful than the majority of managers.

This book challenges you to be what you can be, and (I cannot emphasize enough) one that expects you to be "smarter than most." So now you have been warned.

If you can deal with power, if you can deal with success, read on. You have the freedom of interpretation, to apply the principles to your work life where they are applicable or to ignore a particular maxim that may not be appropriate for you at the moment you read it. Interpretation of information is a requirement for every worker who strives to be a manager, and for every manager who strives to be a leader.

In the context of this book, organizations can be national or multinational, small or large, divisions or departments. The words and ideas are dynamic, not static. As your particular organizational situation changes, you will gain new meaning from the words and concepts presented, and should apply them to your new situation. A wise manager is eclectic in his thoughts and actions.

Read the book once, set it down for a while, and then read it again. Grasp the easy ideas and put them to use immediately. Think about the more difficult ones and apply them as you gain understanding and confidence in your management ability. By doing these things you will become a success—and an extraordinary manager. Indeed, through the proper application of the maxims you can become a leader.

Truth is elusive, so use caution when searching for it. Action is a necessity, so cling to it. Agree when you find it necessary, curse if you find it comforting, and apply it if you find it fitting.

Acknowledgments

Thanks are always difficult. To thank everyone by name who has given assistance through deed or example would take another volume. To include the world would be presumptuous; to include no one would be parsimonious. So these are just a few who deserve praise, not blame. I think it is standard to say the errors are mine and not theirs. Indeed, they are.

This would not be a book without the efforts of the ancients. So I appreciate the original thoughts of Niccolò Machiavelli (1469–1527) in his writings, *The Prince, The Discourses On The First Ten Books of Titus Livy,* and *The Art of War*, and Titus Livy (59 B.C. – A.D. 17) for his narrative of the history of Rome.

I am also grateful to the following libraries for their assistance in obtaining books from their special collections: the University of Tulsa library, Special Collections, Tulsa, Oklahoma, especially Jennifer Carlson; the Huntington Research library, San Marino, California, especially Virginia Renner; Washington University library, Special Collections, St. Louis, Missouri, especially Cinda Ann May.

A special thanks to: Praeger Publishers for their support and confidence in publishing this book; my editor, Jim Dunton, for his guidance, encouragement, and support; Bert Yaeger, project editor, and Kathryn Follett, copy editor; as well as Tom Power for his enthusiasm about my original manuscript.

And I am grateful to and thankful for my family and friends without whom nothing is possible, and the many thoughts that my former teachers and mentors at all levels shared with me. Among the most important was one given to me by my high-school cross-country coach, Coach Barham. He said that the most important thing is not winning a race, but never quitting a race, that quitting is a habit. Once you do it the first time it is easier the next. In writing this book I slowed down once in a while, but I never quit.

I also wish to thank Dr. Dale Johnson of The University of Tulsa, whose guidance in my doctoral studies has assisted me in many projects, including this book; my former students, many of whom taught me, all of whom provided inspiration; my former subordinates, both the motivated and the unmotivated, the caring and the caustic, each gave something; my fellow students and professors, who provided a special learning environment during my MBA studies at Southern Methodist University, where I first encountered the thoughts of Machiavelli; my colleagues and allies, as well as my adversaries and opponents, from many different organizations in both business and politics, each of whom helped in a different way; finally, to those special persons to whom I owe more than words can say—not just for help with this book but with all the rest.

Machiavelli on Management

Introduction

The world of organizations is complex and all encompassing. Most individuals involved in their various corporate roles view life as an "I Win–You Lose" proposition.

Organizations exist in the public and private sectors, in profit and not-for-profit environments, in voluntary and work-for-money situations. Each of these different types of organizations differs in terms of goals, staffing, and other variables, yet the problems of achieving organizational power, and many times individual survival, are found in each of them. Power and survival are constants, found in all organizations worldwide.

In all situations in which a group of people set out to achieve objectives through their organized efforts there exist turf fights, status scrimmages, and too often, destruction of the organization. Individual managers, workers, and work groups make advances and retreats. And in some cases, from an organizational point of view, they commit both murder and suicide.

Even knowing all this, one of the paramount realizations about organizations is that, in reality, we do not understand them very well at all on any long-term basis. Pseudo-solutions come and go, but problems continue. In the aftermath of organizational clashes, there remain the complex dynamics between and among members of the organization, both within their individual work groups and between work groups throughout the organization. On the wider scale, there also exist a variety of inter- and intraorganizational rivalries between and among different organizations.

Size is not a factor when it comes to people striving for power. Corporate conflict is present in both small and large organizations, as well as national and multinational corporations. Nor is the number of people belonging to an organization important for wars and rumors of wars. All that is needed for a good clash is two or more people—each seeing his views as right and his opponents' views as wrong.

Among the management enlightenments of the last century are the pronouncements of a multitude of organizational principles that are supposed to work most of the time, and theories of management and supervision that are supposed to work some of the time. While these erudite pronouncements are important, they have not been successful in lessening the stress on individuals involved in the pursuit of organizational objectives.

University students of management study these principles to take them into the real world, and practitioners of management are exposed to them in training classes and workshops with the purported purpose of increasing productivity. However, all you need do is talk to a practicing manager in an organization to find that all the theories have serious shortcomings when the manager attempts to put them into actual practice. They are often equivocal, and they rarely work as planned. You only need to talk to employees of any organization to discover that their organization does not always practice what it preaches, nor do their managers always do what they have been taught. The workshops attended by managers, at a cost of thousands of organizational dollars, neither enable them to effectively control employees and staff, nor keep them from using power in an illegitimate and abusive manner.

In the search for true management principles, it is important to realize that managers will always resist attempts to change their behavior and that, for the survival of an individual in an organization, it is necessary to see through their facades and deal with them in the light of reality.

Organizational people spend their time talking about and building kingdoms, controlling empires, playing corporate politics, making power plays, kicking someone up or out of the organization, searching for excellence, and being number one. These words are synonymous with the present-day philosophy of being efficient and effective, of increasing productivity, of making a profit, or of being philanthropic. They are primitive words, which act as substitutes for the one word for what most would agree organizations are established to do—survive. They are not intrinsically evil unless the motivations behind them are encompassed in an environment of corruption and deceit—as these motivations often are.

It is then that you need to understand, not the art of management, but the art of survival. And that need for survival is translated from the organization to the individual—indeed, to your own survival. Too often the two are not harmonious. Thus clashes arise, and when they involve an individual against an organization, generally the organization is more adept at surviving. Certainly many times the survival of individuals or groups of individuals within an organization is decided by the whims of a few.

The dissonance that the necessity for survival creates, results in partisan action, and feigned cooperation between managers and workers. The struggle clearly becomes one of us against them. It is seldom that managers ever advocate a reduction of managerial staff so that more workers can be hired, nor do labor leaders propose hiring less labor in exchange for higher technology. The consistent thought is, "I am first, you are second." The needs of the organization become subordinate to the needs of the individuals.

The purpose of this book is not to repudiate or disparage the pronouncements of others, nor to establish rote rules of survival or principles of management. The purpose is to demonstrate principles and rules of organizational life that managers, would-be-managers, and the employees of managers can live by, instead of the masks that cause job heartache, job loss—and sometimes worse.

However, it is a survival book. It is not a book about how others survived, but about how you can survive. It is a book about gaining legitimate power and using that power creatively in order to be the best in the organization, for the organization.

It is written for students of management and active practitioners of management at every level who want to be a success.

It is for those managers and employees who sometimes feel the flames of organizational survival at their feet.

It is written for those who tend to be unhappy because organizational rules and policies say one thing and their managers do the opposite.

It is written for the legions of people who depend on goods and services produced by organizations. Most public organizations are established to serve you, and for you to effectively demand the best from them— good customer service—it helps to understand how they and those who manage them function.

It is also written for corporate shareholders, whose job it is to assure that management carry out its responsibility to them, and for boards of directors who have not been active in management, so that they can understand what goes on behind the scenes—and thus better control the actors.

The activities of organizations are often ambiguous and threatening. Indeed, they are difficult to comprehend and impossible to conquer without at least a modicum of understanding of their nature and purpose. Therefore, the more you understand, the less dangerous the organization and organizations you interact with can become to you. And if the ubiquitous "it and they" continue to be your enemy—then the better you understand the rules, the better you can do battle.

It is nonunderstanding of "real" organizational rules that causes heart-ache, forms of psychosis, organizational stress, and a multitude of other psychological and physiological problems to individuals both within and outside the organization. Indeed, as we approach the twenty-first century, that "collective" stress has become a plague on the modern-day world.

So it is with these purposes in mind that you can learn from the thoughts of Niccolò Machiavelli, a sixteenth-century Florentine nobleman who was both a statesman and student of effective leadership. And while Machiavellian concepts are at times thought synonyms for shrewdness and cunning—in a nonvalue sense—he had many ideas that can be translated into working rules for survival in today's business organizations, just as Aristotle had many ideas that are translated into modern-day living.

However, you cannot "just read" Machiavelli's words, which were written in the environment of sixteenth-century political life; his words must be interpreted in the context of today's corporate world. Machiavelli's *The Prince*, *The Art of War*, and *The Discourses on Titus Livy* give multiple illustrations of every type of modern-day organization. And within them can be found the prescription for proper courses of action by those who seek to be successful managers.

Machiavelli's purpose of writing was not to be revolutionary nor radical, but to describe situations in terms of what they were and not what they should have been. He was an organizational pragmatist. The political situations he described are closely akin to the corporate situations in today's world. Corporate atrocities are not carried out with the sword, but with the pink slip or the lateral transfer.

It is only by gleaning from the ideas of management writers (Abraham Maslow, Douglas McGregor, Peter Drucker, Karl Weick, et al.) that Machiavelli's works can be used in a sensible, logical fashion. Rather than a quantum leap, throughout the past several centuries gradual steps have been taken that provide the stage in which Machiavellian thought can be translated into management thought.

In the search for management excellence, it is critical to learn how to obtain power and use it effectively and efficiently. This is important because power is a necessity in all organizational endeavors and all group activity. It is the glue that holds diverse and conflicting ideas together. Power gives direction to the random impulses of the individual members. Indeed, it is the *Urstoff*—the vital force—of organizations. Power can be used for both good and evil. However, power is not something that should be destroyed because it has an evil side, but something that should be cultivated because of the good it can be used to achieve.

Power is a reality of organizational life, and if you don't acquire it, someone else will. So the question is not, Should there be power in an organization? but, Who will have the power and how should it be managed effectively, efficiently, and creatively?

In this quest, it is important to make a clear distinction between managers who are cruel, who may emulate some of Machiavelli's principles, and what I have called the real Machiavellian managers—the Theory M managers. The former care little for employees and are conspicuously egotistical; they are, in fact, cruel for the sake of being cruel. The latter follow Machiavellian principles out of concern for themselves, their employees, and their organization—always in the proper mix. They create an environment in which their staffs and employees can become more successful and their organizations can reach greater heights. While often misunderstood because of tactics they must employ for organizational success, their value to their staffs and organizations is immensely greater than that of cruel managers or of the traditional Theory X and Theory Y managers.

While some will seek the insight into power shown in this book for their own selfish interest, others will desire it so that they will gain a greater understanding of themselves and can lead others to a better understanding of themselves and to greater prosperity as organization members. The cruel manager's paradigm of power is one of unashamed greed and unambiguous evil, but the paradigm of the Theory M manager is one of generosity and justice. To reiterate, it is not the effective use of power that is bad, but rather the misuse of power. Or as Alexis de Tocqueville said, "It is not exercise of power or habits of obedience which deprave men, but the exercise of a power which they consider illegitimate and obedience to a power which they think usurped and oppressive."

I have named these enlightened managers—leaders—whether CEOs, presidents, front-line supervisors or team leaders, "manager/princes." In their struggle for organizational success, they win because they fight from a position of both intellectual and physical strength. They use power effectively, efficiently, and creatively in order to achieve the greatest organizational good—the organizational summum bonum.

No doubt some can and will misinterpret the rules espoused in this book and use them unfavorably in the conduct of their affairs and the affairs of their work groups or organizations. There always have been those who misused good ideas, but by knowing the rules you can know when they have misbehaved, and perhaps what action you should take. And if the rules and principles are subject to misuse, then it is to everyone's advantage to understand what the misusers are doing. It is by the pronouncement of Theory M, and the prescribing of rules, if put into action by you, that will enable you to counteract and hold the misusers in check. With this enlightened understanding of power, managers and workers alike can truly gain control of themselves and their organizations.

With the publishing of this book, it is time for organization members to accept responsibility for their actions and stop talking about ''it and they'' as if they were not a part of the problem or the solution. It is now time for leaders to lead with confidence and concern for all those under their direction. Machiavelli said it best:

[V]ictories are never so complete that the victor can disregard all considerations whatsoever, . . . especially . . . [the need for justice],

(The Prince: 167)

[w]henever either [managers or organizations] are afraid lest their [staffs] should revolt, it results mainly from the hatred of the [staffs] on account of the bad treatment experienced from those who [manage] them; and this comes either from the belief that they can best be controlled by force, or from lack of sound judgment in [managing] them.

(The Discourses: 293)

1
The Nature of Organizations

For to undertake the [management] of conquered [organizations] by violence, especially when they have been accustomed to the enjoyment of liberty, is a most difficult and troublesome task; and unless you are powerfully armed, you will never secure their obedience nor be able to govern them.

(The Discourses: 238)

To be able to utilize power effectively and reach the goals you have set for yourself, you must first understand the nature of organizations and how you and your organization fits in the "big picture."

IN THE BEGINNING

All businesses and organizations that have held power over the general public either have their beginnings within multi-generational success or entrepreneurial fortune. Multinational organizations, closely held family businesses or tightly controlled public corporations are only branches of trees the economic roots of which were planted hundreds of years ago.

In other words, those who made it during the Industrial Revolution are the ones who are making it today. They are the ones with the power, and if you did not have a great-grandfather as a robber baron or just a plain business robber, then your future success within an organization can only be guaranteed if you become an entrepreneur. This can be done either by developing an entrepreneurial spirit within an established organization or by creating a new organization—and by gaining power and using it with passion—compassionately the majority of the time but ruthlessly when necessary. Machiavelli recognized the need for the use of force in acquiring power and advised the prince as he would advise you today:

[Organizations] thus acquired have either been used to live under a Prince or have been free; and he who acquires them does so either by his own arms or by the arms of others, and either by good fortune or by valor.

(The Prince: 1)

What Machiavelli said was that if luck or special ability is lacking in your pursuit of power and position, then force becomes a necessity. If an opponent is not ready to concede victory to you on the organizational field of battle, then you must be ready to take it by force—by playing and winning power games.

Types of Organizations

This is true whether your organization is public or private, proprietorship or a partnership, or for profit or not for profit. Although once any organization is analyzed it is readily seen that at the beginning there is always one person who is not afraid to take a chance and to channel the use of power toward his goals. This is the founder, who is the beginning—the root—of every great organization. After the founder are the successful managers who become the leaders of the organization. At the Ford Motor Company there are no more opportunities to be Henry Ford.

Changing Times

As we approach the twenty-first century we see that the world is rapidly changing. The battles and wars that were once fought in life or death struggles on the field of battle are now fought in corporate boardrooms. The captains of cavalry are now captains of industry. The generals' decisions are no longer about capturing hills and valleys but about seizing new markets; they are not about the treatment of prisoners of war but about the treatment of those affected by a corporate takeover. And while the results may not be immediate physical life or death, these economic battles can cause real psychological and physical damage to the players that actually can result in real death.

The power used in these battles is not rated in the number of cavalry or the megatonnage of rockets and bombs but in the size of work forces and the effectiveness of managers. And the results of the use of this power are not measured in terms of the number of the enemy killed or captured or real estate gained, but in the number of dollars, yen, or marks gained or lost—or by some other monetary indicator.

THE BIG PICTURE

Indeed it is important for your success to have an understanding of what the big picture looks like and where you fit within it. As the world becomes more complex, the economic actions of a single company in one country affect the well-being of companies in other countries. With enterprise-wide computing, and other high-tech advancements, these effects are now felt immediately, not quarters or years in the future.

And when assessing the power of a nation's business organizations, it is found that the total property and business rights that are collectively held are fairly stable. This measurement is usually expressed as gross national product (GNP) or some other economic indicator. However, this measurement of goods and services produced by a nation does not account for the business rights and power acquired through successful management practices or lost through bad management practices. And it is this measurement of management power that gives true value to a company, an industry or a nation.

While politicians and business leaders discuss the potential consequences of global takeovers, the results of these takeovers are more than changes in the management styles of managers in different countries. Global takeovers result in the gaining or losing of economic power—and thus real power—by a nation. And the proper way of measuring those changes is not by determining the nationality of most of the managers or workers in a company, nor by who the CEO is. The correct way is by observing after the takeover dust settles who the key decision makers are—who takes orders from whom, who has the real power, who are the subordinate managers and who are the decision makers—in other words, who won the power game. And as the results of global takeovers trickle down through a society, they will eventually affect the life-styles of all of its people.

The ultimate measurement of a nation's success, then, is not only its GNP or some other economic indicator, but who owns the final decision in the management decision-making process. This is what determines who will control world markets and what the definition of good and bad management will be. It is only the powerful who survive these competitive environments, whether they be nations, companies, divisions, or individual managers. And this allocation of power will ultimately control the destiny of every union and every management association—and of every worker in every organization.

International Takeovers

When an industry of one nation buys a company or dominates an industry in a foreign nation, it also is acquiring power in the form of managerial expertise. Since this expertise is a scarce resource, the more one nation can capture and use another's managerial expertise, the more it is able to increase its own nation's productivity.

Therefore, if one nation aspires to economic superiority over another, it is important that it maintain a lead in managerial power, either by developing its work force to be more effective and efficient managers or by buying the managers of the other country. And unlike a nation's armed forces or military secrets, its management expertise can be bought. It does not have to be bought through covert deeds but can be purchased in the open for all to view.

Industry Takeovers

This same takeover principle is true for an individual organization within a single nation's industry. The organization that has the greater quantity of high-caliber managers will be more successful than its competitors. Therefore, if your organization is to be successful in enlarging its market or in taking over other organizations, it must increase its power by recruiting and retaining a team of managers par excellence—and then giving them an elite work force and equipping them with the best technology available.

Success through Understanding

While this big picture—the macroenvironment—is confusing to many organizations and individual managers, it is those who thoroughly understand it who become successful at the microlevel. The person who understands the value of a penny will acquire the most dollars. But conversely it is the manager who understands the grand scheme of the organizational world who will acquire the most power within his organization. Therefore, as you begin your journey to success through the use of power, don't overlook the big picture.

PUTTING YOURSELF IN THE PICTURE

Nevertheless, while *global power* is complex and changes with the passing of time, the main fact of power you need to concentrate on as you begin your journey to success is that *managerial power* is relatively constant within your professional lifetime. It is the extraordinary manager who is able to create an abundance of new management power that will last past his lifetime. And as Machiavelli aptly pointed out, those who do create excess power often do so at their own peril.

[I]f the history of [the Roman Emperors] were carefully studied, it would prove an ample guide to any [manager], and serve to show him the way to glory or to infamy, to security or to perpetual apprehension. For of the twenty-six . . . that reigned from the time of Caesar to that of Maximinius, sixteen were assassinated, and ten only died a natural death.

(*The Discourses*: 124)

Therefore, in your journey toward success it is not vital to create new power but only to acquire the power of others, power that is already available in every organization. So if you choose not to emulate Caesar in organizational death and if you are interested in your long-term survival, do not acquire so much power that you become the target of others who lust for power. Short-term success does not necessarily mean long-term happiness.

Acquiring the Power of Others

It is not power itself but the transferring of these rights to power and the production of new power, however limited, that account for the struggles between workers and managers and among the managers of an organization. Therefore, if you are to be a wise manager, it is important that you maximize the amount of power that you have within your organization by securing power from your opponents for yourself and your organization.

However, in doing this you should make your position so strong that others would never dream to attack it. It is just as true today as it was in Machiavelli's day that, *only the strong survive.*

. . . to found a [organization] which should endure a long time it would be best to organize her internally . . . or to locate her . . . in some strong place; and to make her sufficiently powerful, so that no one could hope to overcome her readily, and yet on the other hand not so powerful as to make her formidable to her neighbors.

(*The Discourses*: 112–13)

Organizational Growth

The quantity of property an organization or an individual has is the manifestation of the power they hold. Therefore, in order for your organization to grow and for you to become a successful manager, it is necessary to develop or annex the maximum possible amount of property—goods, services, work force, and so on. And as I have pointed out,

since the creation of new power is difficult and full of hazard, to increase
your power, it is of greater benefit to annex the property rights of other
organizations or of other managers.

Ask any takeover king if it is easier to build, or take what someone else
has built. Ask the Japanese if it is easier to develop an industry or buy
a successful one.

This takeover of existing power is more easily accomplished by a successful joining of forces or merger of two or more organizations. And of
course, after the joining, the destruction of some of the joined forces. The
only acceptable result for you afterwards is that your organization—be
it the whole company or a division within the whole—be the surviving
one. Let someone else worry about starting a new business or about
outplacement. But to accomplish this, you must be both wise and powerful, and when you play power games your power must always be greater
than that of your opponents.

KNOW YOUR STRENGTH

Before beginning any type of organizational battle, you must measure
both your power and that of your opponents. If you find an opponent's
position stronger than yours, it is wise to follow the advice of Machiavelli:

All those who are dissatisfied with their ruler should . . . measure and weigh
well their strength, and if sufficiently powerful to be able to declare themselves
his enemies, and to make open war . . . they should take that course as the least
dangerous and most honorable. But if their condition be such that their forces
do not suffice for open war . . . then they should seek by every art to win his
friendship, and for this purpose employ all possible means, such as adopting his
tastes, and taking delight in all things that give him pleasure. Such intimacy will
insure you tranquillity without any danger, and enable you to share the enjoyment of the prince's good fortune with him, and at the same time afford you
every convenience for satisfying your resentment.

(*The Discourses*: 324)

In other words, *Measure your opponents' strength and attack them only when
yours is sufficient to win. Otherwise, become their friend so as to enjoy their
success—until such time as your power is greater.*

Takeovers

Takeover of any type of organization can only be accomplished successfully by acquiring enough capital assets to sustain a battle, through
the hiring of mercenaries—skilled attorneys, accountants, and so on—
and putting them in place by using your total managerial skill, and your

power. The less capital assets you have, the more power you need. If capital assets are equal or not an issue, then it is only the use of power that counts.

In playing power games you should concentrate only on your objectives, employing those tactics or maneuvers that are necessary to achieve your goals. Any concessions or retreats made in the process of takeovers must be only temporary resting points. On your journey toward management success you must use whatever devices are necessary to achieve your objectives. If you reach obstacles you should consolidate your gains and rearrange your plans—but then proceed upon your course toward success with vigor.

Who Is Number One?

In your quest toward success—your journey to becoming the best—it is important to be self-assured and not to be overly dependent on others. Rarely can you depend on others to draw your battle plans or to fight the management wars that are necessary for ensuring your victory. In working with other managers, employees,and staff, it is necessary to be cautious because their interest, not yours, prevails, and you must monitor their actions closely and carefully. As Machiavelli said,

It is an ignoble resource, since it does not depend on you for its success; and those modes of defense are alone good, certain, and lasting, which depend upon yourself and your own worth.

(*The Prince*: 182)

And while luck and technical talent can at times help you in becoming more successful or in gaining more resources and more organizations, don't depend on them. Use luck and talent as elements of a power game, but not as the only elements. Indeed, if you are to become a success, you must be ever mindful to seize the moment, making luck your ally, not your foe. But since these happenings are limited within the scope of your career, if you plan and wait only for lucky opportunities, you will usually find yourself conquered by those who are more mindful of true opportunities—those who are prepared not only to seize the moment but to help make the moment.

You can again find wisdom in the thoughts of Machiavelli:

[M]en who are to [accomplish] any thing are first to learn which way it is to be done [to play power games] that they may afterwards be the more able to [put it into operation when the occasion arises].

(*The Art of War*: 521)

If you are a wise manager you will wait for the right moment, helping to create it when appropriate, and then seize it when it arrives. You will always find victory in defeat and happiness in victory. The obstacles to achieving your goals will only be challenges that you meet with enthusiasm. When Appius, an up-and-coming Roman, attempted a takeover, those who opposed him put obstacles in his way.

And as they feared to oppose him openly, they resolved to do it by artifice. [They gave] him the authority to propose the future Ten to the people, believing that he would observe the practice of others to whom this confidence has been shown, and not propose himself, which was regarded in Rome as an improper and ignominious thing to do. "But he, in fact, converted the 'impediment' into his opportunity," and did not hesitate to nominate himself as the very first, to the astonishment and disgust of all the nobles; and then he nominated nine others to suit himself.

(*The Discourses*: 183)

2
Corporations and Long-lived Enterprises

For since a Prince by birth has fewer occasions and less need to give offense, he ought to be better loved, and, unless outrageous vices make him odious, will naturally be popular with his subjects. Moreover, the mere antiquity and continuance of his rule will [erase] the memories and causes which lead to innovation. For one change always leaves a [platform] on which another can be built.

(*The Prince*: 3)

The power that organizations need to survive the test of time is gained by changing the faces of managers, but not the face of management policy. New managers bring new ideas to an organization, while old managers get caught in the rut of not changing to meet new demands. In order to retain managers with experience and to maintain their loyalty, it is worthwhile not to dismiss experienced managers in order to acquire new managers, but to transfer them to new positions within a company.

The policies a company develops and follows can assure that management changes are productive, not disruptive, and by managers showing allegiance to established policies—policies that have proven to be valid—a tradition is developed within an organization that gives employees confidence in the stability of the company and gives consistency to the changing faces of its managers. These "traditional" policies should be global in nature and deal with goals and objectives. They should be statements of the purposes of the organization and are not mere sets of procedures.

If new managers respect these policies, they will acquire some of the prestige that the previous managers earned.

LONG-LASTING ORGANIZATIONS

While at times the rules and regulations of governments cheat the perpetuity of family organizational control through enforcement of restrictive tax laws, and while management bloodlines die, either through lack of proper training in the art of management or through misfortune, the laws of incorporation granted by states—which have been created by the management class—are a method of ensuring organizational survival. The long-lasting organization is the one that can be inherited, or continued, easily. Because of their perpetuity, they are usually greater than the ones that fade away with the demise of their founder.

For organization survival and success it is necessary that managers be astute, not just in maintaining the legal structure so that it can be passed to their children, or surrogate children—management trainees, junior partners, shareholders—but in establishing an environment in which the organization can grow and prosper.

ESTABLISHED ORGANIZATIONS

In managing an established organization, a manager must keenly understand the rituals of previous managements, especially the true goals of the founder(s)—not just those that are openly stated. If these true goals are shrouded in company policy or meaningless mottos, then the manager should study the life-style and driving forces of the founder(s), and those of other original managers in the organization. This will assist him in gaining a proper perspective on his own limited role in the total life of the management of the organization; and this enlightened perspective will help him in gaining success by allowing him to understand that it is important for him to achieve not only the goals of the organization, but his individual goals.

If the founders' intents are hidden, then he should trace as far back as possible the real intent of organization policies and rules. And it is critical that he understand that the fundamental purpose of an organization is to serve people—employees and customers. When this principle is violated, the managers and their organization will crumble. Of if the organization itself does not crumble, it will succeed through the efforts of others—the ones who took the ineffective managers' place.

Princes should remember, then, that they begin to lose their [organization] from the moment when they begin to disregard the laws and ancient customs under which the people have lived contented for a length of time.

(*The Discourses*: 328)

Greatness from Others

By studying the past, a manager can embody within himself the trappings of all original legitimate power within the organization. By learning the appropriate management style, he can display to his subordinates a semblance of the ancient power. And by building upon the experiences and successes of others, the manager can maintain the illusion that he deserves the respect that was given to previous managers. He can acquire success by emulating what other successful managers have done.

For since men for the most part follow in the footsteps and imitate the actions of others, yet cannot adhere exactly to those paths which others have taken, or attain to the virtues of those whom they would resemble, the wise man should always follow the roads that have been trodden by the great, and imitate those who have most excelled, so that if he cannot reach their perfection, he may at least acquire something of its savor.

(*The Prince*: 31)

And it is key in gaining this success that a manager always maintain at least a modicum of original legitimate power.

Traditions

A manager also needs to study the traditions and successes of organizations that his organization is competing with. For by learning about their origins and the nature of their management, he can ward off future attacks.

Roots

If you give the roots of tradition their proper place in your development toward a personal style of leadership, by exceeding generally acceptable norms and by meeting the reasonable expectations of subordinates, you will be able to cope with the eventual unforeseen tragedies that await every manager.

[Y]ou may find that you have enemies in all those whom you have injured in seizing the [organization], yet cannot keep the friendship of those who helped you to gain it; since you can neither reward them as they expect, nor yet, being under obligations to them, use violent remedies against them.

(*The Prince*: 5)

And by giving recognition to symbols such as the company Christmas bonus or the time-honored gold retirement watch, the contemporary manager will win the respect of those whom he wishes to lead. If he ever loses his organization through some unforeseen action by the board of directors, stockholders, or unions, the manager will more easily regain it again, and take his proper place as manager/prince.

[H]ereditary [organizations], accustomed to the family of their [manager], are maintained with far less difficulty than new [organizations], since all that is required is that the [manager] shall not depart from the usages of his ancestors, trusting for the rest to deal with events as they arise . . . . [He] will always maintain himself in his Princedom, unless deprived of it by some extraordinary and irresistible force; and even if so deprived will recover it, should any mishap overtake the usurper.

(*The Prince*: 2–3)

RIGHTFUL MANAGERS

In as much as rightful managers, not only established managers who have already acquired a great deal of power, but those with a positive mental attitude, have less cause and less necessity to offend other managers and subordinates, it is only natural that they be more cared for and that employees work harder for them. These managers should not make themselves despised by inflicting upon others unnecessary hardship, nor should they show an overly stated appearance of greed.

If they maintain an attitude of being the best and behaving as if they are the best, it is only natural for their subordinates to be loyal. Any memories employees hold of policy changes that displeased them or firings during the period over which these managers had to be forceful in acquiring their power will soon be forgotten.

[I]ll-employed cruelties are those which from small beginnings increase rather than diminish with time. [Those who follow this method will find their condition desperate.]

(*The Prince*: 62–63)

If as a manager you establish a solid foundation within your organization and then build on that foundation, you will greatly increase your chances of success.

Change brings about change. Power brings about power.

3

Takeovers, Consolidation, and Centralization

A prince or a republic that [attacks] another country is satisfied merely to kill its chiefs, but when an entire people aims to possess itself of a country and to live upon that which gives support to its original inhabitants, it must necessarily destroy them all.

(*The Discourses*: 246)

It is the new manager, though he may be seasoned in other business ventures, who suffers the greatest risk in acquiring control and gaining power over new organizations, departments, or divisions. The challenges are not technical, as in manufacturing, product delivery, or delivery of services, but are instead found in confrontations with subordinates or new work groups.

During restructuring or other organizational upheavals, one tactic used against management by employees to better their positions is for them to seek new managers. Workers and unions often rebel in order to acquire managers who will increase their own power base, in the name of seeking better managers. However, experience shows that these rebels never fare better in the long run.

MANAGEMENT SUCCESSION

Whether a management succession has positive results or brings a catastrophe for the organization depends more on the nature of both the previous and successor managers, not just on who the new manager is. If a successful manager is succeeded by another successful manager, then good things can be accomplished, not because of the acts of the workers but because of the virtue of the managers.

[I]f one [manager] succeeds another of equally great abilities and courage, then it will often be seen that they achieve extraordinary greatness for their [organization], and that their fame will rise to the very heavens.

(The Discourses: 147)

In the cases where a successful manager is replaced by a bad or weak manager, subordinates will find that the bad manager is not only more treacherous and deceitful, but that because of his stilted vision, by which he thinks himself to be more favored than a previous manager, his treachery is most often unpredictable and unjust. In order for an organization to prosper, and in turn meet the objectives of the workers, managers must be successful even in their treacheries.

If an able and vigorous [manager] is succeeded by a feeble one, the latter may for a time be able to maintain himself; but if his successor be also weak, then the latter will not be able to preserve his [organization].

(The Discourses: 146)

When acquiring a new organization you cannot depend upon the loyalties of those whom you have injured in the climb to becoming a successful manager, regardless of whether you are taking over a new division, a department, or the whole company—even when your ascent is purported to be for the good of all. It is a foolish manager who measures the value of a merger in any terms less than the advantages either he or his organization achieves.

TAKEOVER TACTICS

When acquiring organizations a manager should be sure he has planned his assault well. The tactics used in the offensive should always be preplanned. One useful tactic is to portray the takeover as entirely for the good of the organization being taken over. This will cause the opposition to lower its defenses and become more susceptible to the takeover. For example, you could facilitate a takeover by letting your aides ''leak'' information about the benevolent attitudes of the management attempting the takeover or the news that special benefits will accrue to the managers in the target organization.

[Y]ou will always find . . . men who are discontented and desirous of change, you may readily procure an entrance by gaining over some Baron of the Realm. Such persons . . . are able to open the way to you for the invasion of their country and to make its conquest easy. But afterwards the effort to hold your ground involves you in endless difficulties, as well in respect of those who have helped you, as of those whom you have overthrown.

(The Prince: 25)

PROTECT YOURSELF FROM HARM

After any type of takeover or management change, it is often necessary to destroy those you have conquered, especially if you define them as potential successors or rivals. This is because they will eventually have no loyalty to you, and through their own weaknesses in losing the battle, are worthy of little respect or trust.

[M]en are either to be kindly treated, or utterly crushed, since they can revenge lighter injuries, but not graver. Wherefore the injury we do a man should be of a sort to leave no fear of reprisals.

(The Prince: 10)

Another tactic is to announce to the workers and managers in the target organization that they have nothing to fear from a management change, that their jobs are secure, and that there will be no layoffs.

[A] captain who besieges a city should strive by every means in his power to relieve the besieged of the pressure of necessity, and thus diminish the obstinacy of their defense. He should promise them a full pardon if they fear punishment, and if they are apprehensive for their liberties he should assure them that he is not the enemy of the public good, but only of a few ambitious persons in the city who oppose it.

(The Discourses: 362)

As this relates to the takeover of a company, it will assist by preventing management from seeking a white knight, or lessen the employees' ambition to purchase the organization for themselves. In terms of internal takeovers, this lessens the resistance of those who will be affected by the change.

[H]e ordered his soldiers, in a voice loud enough to be heard by the Veientes, not to harm those that should be disarmed. This caused [them] to lay down their arms, and the city was taken almost without bloodshed. This example was afterwards imitated by several other generals.

(The Discourses: 364)

When a wise manager conquers divisions or departments in the same organization, or takes spoils from organizations that may be geographically distant from his own, then he must use great skill in deciding how to best consolidate his power. And it is important that the manager make these decisions quickly, and against opponents he must take those preemptive actions that are necessary to ensure his success.

[W]hen a State rebels and is again got under, it will not afterwards be lost so easily. For the Prince, using the rebellion as a pretext, will not scruple to secure himself by punishing the guilty, bringing the suspected to trial, and otherwise strengthening his position in the points where it was weak.

(The Prince: 6)

In dealing with subordinates, especially when they are located in different regions, either geographically or dispersed within the same city, it is important that a manager should always make himself well known to all his subordinates. However, at the same time, he must keep them at a correct social distance. He should live in the town where the majority of his subordinates reside, even if he prefers a different location. By being on the spot, he can see employee problems as they arise and put rapid solutions into effect.

But when [organizations] are acquired in a country differing in language, usages, and laws, difficulties multiply, and great good fortune [as well has hard work] . . . is needed to overcome them. One of the best . . . methods for dealing with such a [organization], is for the [manager] who acquires it to go and dwell there in person, since this will make his tenure more secure and lasting.

(The Prince: 8)

Moreover, the Province in which you take up your [residence] is not pillaged by your officers; the people are pleased to have a ready recourse to their Prince; and have all the more reason if they are well disposed, to love, if disaffected, to fear him. A foreign enemy desiring to attack that State would be cautious how he did so. In short where the Prince resides in person, it will be most difficult to oust him.

(The Prince: 8–9)

After a takeover a manager should refrain as much as possible from using study teams to solve problems. And when used, the credit for the study teams' solutions should be taken by the manager. This will increase the confidence his subordinates have in his abilities, and thereby increase the subordinates' need for him. A manager should be perceived by all who are under his command as wise. He should be able to calm their fears as well as solve their problems. By this, loyalty to the manager is increased.

FORTIFY YOUR POSITION

A manager should not hesitate in his actions to fortify a position by amassing many fronts around him through decentralization of tasks, functions, divisions, or regions. A manager should consider the possible extra expense or loss of profits as an investment in the future. For with decentralization, the manager is able to appoint people as directors, division heads, supervisors, and in other executive positions. These appointments become payments for loyalty and provide control, which will be amortized over his tenure.

And there is often a direct relationship between the ability to give rewards and the loyalty that a manager can expect—although a wise manager should never view this as true loyalty. Certainly a manager must reward well those who have helped him in his journey to a high management position. First he should help those within his original organization who are privy to secrets or plans. However, the wise manager must always have his finger on the pulses of even trusted lieutenants, to make sure they remain loyal.

But where they abstain from attaching themselves to you of set purpose and for ambitious ends, it is a sign that they are thinking more of themselves than of you and against such men a Prince should be on his guard, and treat them as though they were declared enemies, for in his adversity they will always help to ruin him.

(*The Prince*: 68–69)

If a gleam is detected in a lieutenant's eyes that might indicate aspirations contrary to his own, then the manager should be prepared to punish them.

[A] Prince should inspire fear in [such a way] that if he [does] not win love he may escape hate. For a man may very well be feared and yet not hated.

(*The Prince*: 121)

LET SOME FAIL

If a manager can be assured that potential rivals will fail in their efforts, then they should be allowed to stay within the organization, so that through their failures others can see the unsoundness of disloyal actions. Once he has let them fail, and has let that failing be public within the organization, a manager should immediately dismiss them from the organization with great talk of their failing, making sure that other lieutenants are at the same time rewarded.

As you reward your children with praise and admiration to gain their affection, so should you use the same devices for gaining the loyalty of those you need in your climb toward success in management.

THE PATH OF THE FEW

If a manager is powerful enough, willing to do battle, and able to gain allies who are not as strong as he is, he may choose to consolidate his power base through decentralization—either internally or geographically. To do this he should set upon a course that few survive, although they that do are extraordinary. He should attempt to make his organization as large as possible. Not only should he concentrate on internal growth, but he should create new organizations when appropriate and acquire existing ones in order to reach his growth objectives.

The Prince who establishes himself in a [foreign] Province . . . ought also to make himself the head and protector of his feebler neighbors, and seek to weaken the stronger, and must see to it that by no chance shall any other stranger as powerful as himself find entrance there.

(The Prince: 11)

DOMINATION

His goal may be domination of an industry or a market area, or wider domination through the formation of a multinational organization. The multinational or national conglomerate gives a manager the chance to make significant social policy decisions. And these decisions are important not only for the success of organizations in general, but also for the continuation of the management profession.

When amassing large organizations, a manager may display himself as being loosely organized through the method of using many different corporations as well as through decentralization of functions and services. This tactic will assist in preventing opponents—government agencies or public organizations—from claiming that the organization is too powerful and that it should either be more closely regulated or broken into smaller units.

The manager can also instigate a strong public relations campaign to tell of his virtues and of his organization's contribution to the public good. This enables him to strengthen his position by appearing to be weak. People fear and defend themselves against the strong, but open their arms to those they think weak.

Centralize through Decentralization

The only formula that can be used in issuing a plan to centralize through decentralization is to capitalize on the loyalty of those you judge loyal and to scatter to the winds those you know to be disloyal or who have a disloyal disposition. In taking over another organization, those who have been in positions of power and decision making, and those who are capable of creating dissent, must be immediately discharged.

He who is made Prince by the favor of the nobles, has greater difficulty to maintain himself than he who comes to the Princedom by aid of the people, since he finds many about him who think themselves as good as he, and whom, on that account, he cannot guide or govern as he would. But he who reaches the Princedom by the popular support, finds himself alone, with none, or but a very few about him who are not ready to obey.

(*The Prince*: 66–67)

Whence we may draw the general axiom, which never or rarely errs, that he who is the cause of another's [gaining power] is himself undone, since he must work either by craft or force, each of which excites distrust in the person raised to power.

(*The Prince*: 21)

Spies Needed during Takeovers

When taking over other organizations it may be necessary for a manager to have someone in his organization to covertly infiltrate the opposition in order to learn the true thoughts of the losers.

Another excellent expedient is to send colonies into one or two places, so that these may become, as it were, the keys of the Province; for you must either do this, or else keep up a numerous force of men-at-arms and foot soldiers.

(*The Prince*: 9)

When decentralizing a manager should never decentralize to the degree that loyal workers and staff are isolated in a hostile situation, nor should they be placed in a conquered organization without enough staff or authority to rid the organization of the conquered management. On the other hand, they should not be given authority to such a degree that they will neither have to strive for your organizational goals nor pledge their loyalty, in both words and actions, to other organizations.

The worst that a Prince need fear from a disaffected people is, that they may desert him, whereas when the nobles are his enemies he has to fear not only that they may desert him, but also that they may rebel against him; because, as they have greater craft and foresight, they always are in time to save themselves, and seek favor with the side they think will win.

(*The Prince*: 67)

Anticipating Problems

In order to be assured of organizational success, it is critical that a manager not only consider present problems but anticipate future ones.

For the [disorders of an organization] being discovered while yet inchoate, which can only be done by a [wise] ruler, may be dealt with; but when, from not being observed, they are suffered to grow until they are obvious to everyone, there is no longer any remedy.

(The Prince: 13–14)

This is aided by using participative devices. Suggestion boxes for employees, ample time off, workshops, and company baseball teams are worthwhile devices. At the same time, employees should not be allowed to participate in activities that will give them too much knowledge of the organization. You must use caution allowing them their fair share—giving too little causes hostility; giving too much bolsters equality—and both traits can be counterproductive to your goals. Regardless of your posture you will always be given quality time by some employees who believe that the greatest reward is to help the organization succeed, regardless of the personal cost. In deciding upon the degree of participation to use, you should follow the maxim of participative management: Never use *only* participative management, but use the devices when they are to your advantage.

Make Yourself Known

In a highly decentralized organization, where departments or divisions may be many miles or even continents apart, it is critical that a leader never be forgotten. The employees should consistently be alerted to his successes both within and outside the organization. A manager should visit all the sites he is responsible for on at least an annual basis, and if the organization is too large for this he should send one or more of his most trusted aides or a family member in his place.

[I]t greatly profits a Prince in conducting the internal government of his State, to follow striking methods. . . . But above all, he should strive by all his actions to inspire a sense of his greatness and goodness.

(The Prince: 165)

A manager should create a public relations department, the job of which is to constantly sell the employees on the goodness of the organization, and of him. Every office in each location should have a picture of the manager so that the employees will be familiar with him, and thus acquire a distant feeling of friendship.

But he who against the will of the people is made Prince by the favor of the nobles, must, above all things, seek to conciliate the people, which he readily may by taking them under his protection. And since men who are well treated by one whom they expected to treat them ill, feel the more beholden to their benefactor, the people will at once become more devoted to such a Prince when he protects them, than if he owed his Princedom to them.

(The Prince: 69)

Have Those Who Can Speak Well of You

In all situations in which organizational conflict is present, it is more difficult for friends than enemies to arise in opposition to you at the time of battle, be it a vote of stockholders or of a board of directors, or just a vote of confidence by other managers. Therefore, it is always good to have those in your organization who speak well of you.

[I]t is essential for a Prince to be on a friendly footing with his people, since, otherwise, he will have no resource in adversity.

(The Prince: 69–70)

While managing changes, takeovers, and consolidations are filled with danger, if you do all these things not only in a planned manner, but also with the intensity of a sincere heart, you will prevent failures from occurring. It is a weak manager who practices only crisis management; cunning, planning, and wisdom are a much better course.

He who does not manage this matter well, will soon lose whatever he has gained, and while he retains it will find in it endless troubles and annoyances.

(The Prince: 12)

4

Obtaining Power
in an Empire

[Those leaders of old] who . . . desired to preserve their [organiza-
tions studied not only the Art of War but] accustomed themselves,
both minds and bodies to labor, to trouble, and [didn't fear danger]
. . . And though perhaps some of them might be condemned for their
ambition, and [extravagant] desire [for Power]; yet they could never
be accused of [being soft or lazy], or doing anything that might render
them delicate and [gutless].

(The Art of War: 523)

Power is the proximal cause of leadership and the precursor of success
in management. For the manager there are two basic challenges in leading
a group. The first is gaining control; the second is keeping it. And control is only obtainable by having power. The effective use of power can
determine your destiny in an organization.

By using power to control the humans and the machines within your
organization, you are aided in your quest to become a successful manager.
This is true even if you are not the designated manager. For it is possible
for a worker to become a surrogate manager by using power more effectively than the manager. Therefore, the effective use of power can enable
the managed to become the informally recognized manager.

Power is gained by utilizing the skills and talents that you have
previously acquired and by making an inventory of the skills you need
to develop or improve before you begin your quest. Power is fairly constant within an organization, and power that is not held by one person

or group is automatically deferred to another. And power is not always obvious; it may be dormant or active at any given time.

There are two requirements for obtaining power. First, you must desire it. Although there are cases in which people obtain power without first having the desire, these people usually squander the power they have gained, or else over a period of time learn to appreciate the value of power and develop their ability to use it. Next, you must put your power to use.

Power comes in a variety of forms and is called by various names, but effective management of it always produces the same results. The person who has power is the one who is able to select the song that is played at the dance.

REWARD POWER

One method of obtaining power is through the use of rewards. This "reward power" is designated as alpha power. When you reward people for their actions they become more willing to perform in the manner you desire, either because they want more rewards or because they begin to show a genuine affection toward you.

When using reward power or any of the other types of power, it is not your duty to attempt to manipulate the reasons people perform as they do. You are not to be concerned with whether you obtain results because of the former or the latter. Your only interest should be what the results are. Rewards are something your deserving employees have a right to earn. To give rewards only to a particular person or group of employees is not only unwise but contains within it the seeds of your destruction.

The way to [honor] should be open to every citizen, and suitable rewards should be established, that will be satisfactory and honorable to those who merit them. Reputation and influence gained by such pure and simple means will never prove dangerous to any [organization].

(The Discourses: 394)

The value and nature of the rewards depend upon who you are rewarding. You should keep in mind that most people believe it is the giving, not the gift that counts. It is always best to keep the gift or the reward related to the situation and not be pretentious in the giving. Gifts given outside normal giving situations, such as Christmas and birthdays, have greater value than gifts given at those times. While there is sometimes value in blending your gifts with those of others, it is usually better that a gift be directly from you. Gifts in the nature of favors or perquisites that give the person a feeling of being special, or that cannot be given by others, have in them a special intrinsic value. Only the boss can give the subordinate that special day off. And when giving gifts of this type, make sure it is recognized that they are from you and not from the organization. Also, it is always best when gift giving is not ostentatious, and it is very important that it comes from the heart. Indeed, those who truly believe in the pure value of giving receive more power from the giving of rewards and gifts than those who do not give from the heart or are uncertain why gifts are given. This belief is not something that is openly stated but subjectively felt, and understood, by both the giver and the receiver.

The Prince, therefore, who without otherwise securing himself builds wholly on their professions is undone. For the friendships we buy with a price, and do not gain by greatness and nobility of character, though fairly earned are not made good, but fail us when we need them most.

(The Prince: 120)

FORCE POWER

Another method a manager can use to obtain power is threatening or forcing workers to perform tasks in a certain manner. Threat or force power is designated as beta power. As in the use of rewards, use of force as a means for power should be related to the situation. Indeed, using this type of power can result in immediate modifications in the actions of others, although the change obtained is usually not lasting.

Whereas reward power can be used to gain affection, force can result in strained or broken relationships. However, this does not mean you should not use force as part of your recipe for obtaining total power. Neither does it mean force is bad. Oppressive force is bad, but reasonable and necessary force can be good.

Some would have you believe that because at times people do not like to perform certain tasks or perform in a certain manner, that they are reacting to the use of force, when in fact they may be reacting to a wide variety of organizational stimuli. Those who hold this misconception evaluate force only in a negative manner and are blind to its value. However, a wise manager should know from his own feelings that there are times he does not like to do certain things. Therefore, it is only natural that others should occasionally feel this way.

Managers who rely on force power only, or rely on it too often, usually do not involve their staffs in decision making. They fail to use participative devices. It is much easier to motivate subordinates to perform job tasks if they have some input into how the job should be done. Generally speaking, the more force and threats you use, the more often you have to rely on them. Constant use of force and threats results in their losing value as a motivational tool.

Force can be subtle, such as with use of implied threats—"If you don't do this we are all going to be in trouble"—or it can be direct—"If you don't do this by the end of the day you will be fired."

[T]hreats are worse than the execution; in fact, [threats] involve the only danger, there being none in the execution, for the dead cannot avenge themselves, and in most cases the survivors allow the thought of revenge to be interred with the dead.

(The Discourses: 330)

Therefore when using the threat of force you should be extremely judicious. And most important, when you use threats always carry them out. Far worse than having a reputation as a person who makes threats is having a reputation as a person who makes idle threats. As Machiavelli says,

[He] who is threatened, and sees himself constrained by necessity either to dare and do or to suffer, becomes a most dangerous man to the prince.

(The Discourses: 330)

A wise manager will use threats only after much thought and then he will only use them sparingly.

INFORMATION POWER

A third type of power is gained through use of the information or knowledge you hold. Information power is designated as gamma power. To be truly valuable the information should pertain to things needed by those whom you want to influence. While the mere holding of information can result in your gaining a modicum of temporary power, lasting power is only gained by understanding how the information is acquired, what it means, and how it should be used. And for information to be truly valuable, it should be of a type that is constantly renewed or evaluated.

Transient information is that which has little value once it has been given. When you have expended transient information, if that is your only merit, neither it or you have any further value. In an organization this information, or knowledge, power gains greater value when no one or very few others have the same level of knowledge as you have. This knowledge is most often gained through education—either formal or informal—and experience.

While all the various types of power take time to acquire, this is the one for which the necessary prerequisites of knowledge and experience gained over time are the most obvious.

However, knowledge and information do not bring power in and of themselves; those whom you wish to influence with this power must be made aware of it. This is done by the performance of tasks or deeds that no one, or very few, in the organization can do or by making others aware that there are potential problems in the organization that only you can solve, should they occur. Those whom you wish to influence should also be led to believe that the consequences of not solving those problems would bring disaster to the organization.

Employees or staff with an excess of information power can be detrimental to the organization. These are most often the persons who are labeled specialists—whether or not they really are. They often resort to corporate blackmail to gain an advantage over their managers. They make demands on the organization and withhold their knowledge or threaten to withhold their knowledge—often through the threat of quitting—until their demands are met.

To protect from this blackmail by "specialists," managers need a wide variety of experience within organizations, and they need knowledge that enables them to perform a multitude of tasks. If they lack these, then they should know where to find persons who can perform them. Or they should have alternative solutions to the problems that would arise if they lost the specialists' knowledge. It is advisable when forming an organization that an excess of job titles not be created that have the word specialist or expert in them. These titles often lead to employees claiming power to the disadvantage of the manager.

POSITION POWER

A fourth type of power is inherent in the nature of the position you hold. This position, or hierarchical power, is designated as theta power. It is that power which is granted through legal means (express or implied) and gives you the authority to direct the actions of others—by the nature of your position. Within an organization those who have people reporting to them have this power by the nature of their job title, or rank. In small organizations they obtain this power by being the owner or one of the owners of the organization.

By its very nature this power cannot be obtained without having position. It is unique in the fact that it is almost completely external to the holder of the power. While the other types of power depend upon the actions of the person, position power is the result of who the person is. It can be gained by using other types of power.

If the only claim a manager has to power arises from his position, then his power becomes little more than an implied threat. The value of position power is greatly enhanced when a manager is comfortable and confident in his position. This usually takes experience in managing, and the new manager rarely can use position power to its fullest. Those who use position power most effectively wear their position with modesty but understand its depths and know when to bring it to the front.

[A] truly great man is ever the same under all circumstances; and if his fortune varies, exalting him at one moment and depressing him at another, he himself never varies, but always preserves a firm courage, which is so closely interwoven with his character that every one can readily see that the fickleness of fortune has no power over him.

(*The Discourses*: 399–400)

The confidence and presence of the person holding a position always determines the value of this power. If he does not act in a manner that makes him respected by subordinates, then position power is greatly lessened.

[The first way a man is known is] upon the merits of [his] father or relations [and] is so fallacious, that it makes no lasting impression . . . The second, which makes a man known is by the company he keeps, and by his social conduct, is better than the first, but inferior to [the third] which is founded upon his individual actions; for unless a man has by these given some proof of himself, his reputation will depend merely upon public opinion, which is most unstable. But the third course, being founded entirely upon a man's own actions, will from the start give him such a name that it will require a long course of opposite conduct to destroy it.

(*The Discourses*: 407)

Its strength is proportionate to both how high your position is in an organization and your ability to use your position effectively. Its weakness lies in the fact that if you rely on it as your only power when you lose your position you have lost all your power. Therefore in your actions with others you should use your other type powers more often than you use position power.

Therefore when you gain position power, it is very important that you recognize that this is the least valuable of all your powers. If you make it your primary power, it is probable that those over you will use their power to take away your position, or that they will withhold better positions from you through their use of reward and threat power in dealing with you.

BESTOWED POWER

The final type of power available to a manager is the one that should be the goal of all who would be wise managers—your goal—and who desire to claim the title of leader. This is the kind of power bestowed by subordinates on those managers they admire and respect. This bestowed power is designated as omega power. This is legitimate power, and it is rarely if ever oppressive. It is the power that will assist you the most in reaching goals. It is not legitimate just because of rules or policies, but because it is given willingly by your subordinates.

[The manager can avoid or make war at his option] partly by the respect they have for his power, and partly because they are deceived by the means employed to keep them quiet.

(*The Discourses*: 228)

And not only is it not oppressive or suppressive, but it is compassionate and open. Indeed, it is like the light of a candle in the night to show others the way. It causes subordinates to follow a leader willingly, and it enables managers to become leaders.

This power is gained through the use of the correct combination of the other types of power, in the appropriate situations and at the appropriate times. It is power that demands the total discipline of those who would obtain it, and it is available not to the many but to the few. This power cannot be learned in textbooks, but emphasizes the artistic side of a manager and a leader.

CHARISMA

While power has charismatic qualities, a manager does not have to be overtly charismatic to possess it. It is only necessary that a subordinate tacitly recognize an inwardly charismatic personality. And while the allure of the manager might be totally hidden from others, it is the true charisma that is felt by his subordinates, not that which is seen by others, that is important.

5

Games in an Empire

This mode of provoking new wars has always been common amongst potentates, who want at least to make a show of respect for treaties. For if I desire to make war upon any prince with whom I have concluded treaties that have been faithfully observed for a length of time, I shall attack some friend or ally of his under some color of justification, well knowing that, in . . . attacking his friend, he will resent it, and I shall then have grounds for declaring war against him; or, if he does not resent it, he thereby manifest his weakness and lack of fidelity in not defending an ally entitled to his protection. And one or the other of these means will make him lose his reputation, and facilitate the execution of my designs.

(The Discourses: 250)

Games are as much a part of adulthood as they are of childhood, the primary difference being the consequences of winning or losing. And adult organizational games are filled with hazard. Whereas with your monopoly board or scrabble game the rules are conveniently enclosed, when you engage in corporate games there is no preprinted set of rules. And often when playing, the rules the players agree to are changed by one or more of the players. And this is usually done without giving all the players notice—or a new set of rules.

WINNING IS WHAT COUNTS

Before playing organizational games, do not assume that everyone's needs to be happy and satisfied are the same. Throw the dice and bet the chips, knowing that the other players' motives are to win your chips and your power. They intend to win the game, not just to play it. Hence, they often define themselves as right and you as wrong.

And in order to be successful in playing power games, it is necessary to believe in your heart and mind that your winning is for the benefit of everyone, and that the kingdom will be better only if you win. But keep in mind that, however wrong they may be, the other players just might feel the same way.

THE WILL AND SKILL TO PLAY

As in all games, you must develop both the will to play and the skill necessary to win. And in order to be a good player you must play a game that is fun and provides you with enjoyment. Game players who don't enjoy the games they play will often lose to more enthusiastic amateurs.

The will to play is developed by understanding the nature of the benefits gained when you win and the consequences when you lose. And you gain confidence in your play if you are willing to expend energy in pursuing victory. You develop the skill by practicing each of the games until the moves are second nature.

A wise manager plays cautiously and only with others who are of the same skill level. He does not risk too much too soon because he realizes that it is often a series of games, not just one, that is played, and that the winner is determined by who wins most of the games, not all of them.

However, there are times when an individual game or variation of a series of games is a one-time session—the loser really loses. This you will learn not only from playing games yourself, but in watching what happens when others in the organization play similar games. It is always wise to learn from those around you.

You should always be moderate in your play. For example, if the game is one of trying to assume a higher position, do not try to advance many positions all at once unless you are willing to suffer the consequences of losing.

While a wise manager is prepared to win a game at all costs, for the benefit of the many—even the losers—he should not play with such reckless abandon that losing is almost ensured. And above all, when playing power games your goals must be the ones that guide the conduct of the game and formulate and amend the rules as necessary.

BEING A GOOD PLAYER

You can never win a game unless you are a player, so it is important, necessary in fact, to make sure you are available to play. And in order to be a long-term player you must be gracious in both victory and defeat. You must never insult other players, regardless of whether you win or lose.

The use of insulting language towards an enemy arises generally from the insolence of victory, or from the false hope of victory, which latter misleads men as often in their actions as in their words; for when this false hope takes possession of the mind, it makes men go beyond the mark, and causes them often to sacrifice a certain good for an uncertain better.

(The Discourses: 302)

THE GAME OF INSURGENCY

One game that is often played by subordinates, but can also be played by managers, is the game of insurgency.

[F]or the fear to lose stirs the same passions in men as the desire to gain, as men do not believe themselves sure of what they already possess except by acquiring still more; and, moreover, these new acquisitions are so many means of strength and power of abuses.

(The Discourses: 109)

The result, however, is that whenever the enemies of change make an attack, they do so with all the zeal of partisans, while the others defend themselves so feebly as to endanger both themselves and their cause.

(The Prince: 55)

In this game one of the players refuses to do what is asked or required of him. That person in effect is attempting to modify organizational rules and policies. He does not like the rules of the game, and it is in his interest to change them.

[F]or men who are kept in doubt and uncertainty as to their lives will resort to every kind of measure to secure themselves against danger, and will necessarily become more audacious and inclined to violent changes. It is important, therefore, either never to attack any one, or to inflict punishment by a single act of rigor, and afterwards to reassure the public mind by such acts as will restore calmness and confidence.

(The Discourses: 191–92)

However, it is best when playing this game not to totally refuse to do something, but to find a plausible excuse for not doing it. For example, if your job is to move a desk from Floor A to Floor Y, saying the elevator was broken—or breaking the elevator—in order to not be able to move the desk is better than refusing to move the desk. If your job is to have a budget report to a superior by a certain date, it is better to say that the computers that were necessary to prepare the budget were broken than that you did not have time to complete the task.

THE BLAME GAME

In this regard, the less control you have over the obstacles you blame, people or equipment, the better. Yet this is not a necessary rule, because this is not the "blame game," in which the purpose is to blame another manager or unit for the failure to perform a certain task in order to weaken their overall management position.

[T]he first, by denial and by alleging personal hatred to have prompted the accusation; and the other, by denying the charge, and alleging that your accuser was constrained by the force of torture to tell lies.

(*The Discourses*: 338)

THE GAME OF COUNTERINSURGENCY

There are three tactics to use to oppose those who choose to play the game of insurgency.

The first is to tighten controls within the organization. Develop new policies, rules, and procedures to hold the insurgency in check. Begin to use more force and fear power. Because often force and fear will be the only types of power that this type player understands. Let the players know the consequences of continuing to play—hold their feet to the fire.

[While] these people are in a state of stupor and suspense between hope and fear, it behooves you to assure [yourself] either by severity or by bestowing benefits upon them.

(*The Discourses*: 290)

The second is to agree to make the requested change. However, this you must do from a position of strength, not weakness. Your decision to make a change must increase your total power, not the opposition's.

[A]nd this favor was so acceptable to the populace that Rome was wild with joy, thinking it a great benefit, which they had never expected and would not have sought themselves.

(*The Discourses*: 201)

The third is to fight fire with fire. If necessary make a deal with one portion of your staff in order to beat another portion. However, in bargaining never put yourself—or your organization—in a position whereby an employee or group of employees is able to control the operation of the organization.

[T]he loss of independence is a matter of . . . supreme importance to [an organization].

(*The Discourses*: 150)

This can be done in part by creating situations in which units and individuals compete with each other.

[I]t will always be for his interest to keep the state disunited, so that each place and country shall recognize him only as master; thus he alone, and not his country, profits by his conquest.

(*The Discourses*: 231)

It is always harder for competitors to participate in an insurgency than those who have close working relationships and mutual needs.

For [organization] consists mainly in so keeping your subjects that they shall be neither able nor disposed to injure you; and this is done by depriving them of all means of injuring you, or by bestowing such benefits upon them that it would not be reasonable for them to desire any change of fortune.

(*The Discourses*: 289–90)

THE GAME OF SPONSORSHIP

Sponsorship is a game in which you attach yourself—and your fortunes—to one person who will look out for your interest. You can do this either by having only one sponsor or by having a group of sponsors, with one of the group acting as your primary agent. The important objective in this game is to have those who speak well of you. And to be effective the sponsor must be someone higher in the organization who has either formal or informal influence over key decision makers. In essence, you enter into a contract with the sponsors. The agreement is simple. You are loyal to the sponsor; and in exchange the sponsor promotes you and your interest. And while playing this game it is important to be building your own base of support and power. Otherwise, if your sponsor leaves the organization you may find yourself alone.

This game can be played by anyone in the organization; clerks, secretaries, professional staff, middle managers, and in some cases senior-level managers. The main requirement is that your sponsor be significantly higher in the organizational hierarchy than you, unless this person is one who has influence over a person of high rank. For example, it could be the president's secretary or a golfing friend of a board member.

[The Romans] always endeavored to have some friend in these new countries who could aid them by opening the way for them to enter, and also serve as a means for retaining their possessions.

(The Discourses: 229)

THE GAME OF ALLIANCES

In the game of alliances the objective is to build a power base among peers. This may be among managers, professional staff, and at times lower-level persons in the organizations who control the allocation of resources. In essence, agreements are reached in which one player helps another in exchange for support or promised support. The alliance starts with two or more, but it can grow until it can find no more members, is strong enough to dominate issues, or is destroyed either by the formal organization or another alliance. It can be a single-issue alliance (special interest group) or a group that is formed on the basis of personalities and becomes the advocate of many different issues. (Mintzberg: 1983)

Alliances can prove valuable if you choose to play the insurgency game against other managers of your level, or against higher-level managers. It is also possible that the person with whom you form an alliance will also prove valuable in playing the sponsorship game. It is important that you always use caution in selecting allies; however, do not make alliances in which you are totally dependent on others, or in which yours is the subservient position. If you are the dependent person, then the play always begins to your disadvantage. When first playing you may not be able to be as selective as you would like in choosing allies, but by being successful at building early alliances, you can parlay small victories into greater ones. Your goal is to pick allies who recognize your abilities as a leader and defer to most of your decisions.

The second method employed by the ancient republics for their aggrandizement was to make associates of other states; reserving to themselves, however, the rights of sovereignty, the seat of empire, and the glory of their enterprises.

(The Discourses: 238)

THE GAME OF EMPIRE BUILDING

Empire building is one of the oldest games played in organizations. In reality, instead of being a game totally unto itself, empire building is a merger of the other types of games. For in order to build an empire you need alliances, and sponsors from throughout the organization. When playing the empire building game, it is helpful to have responsibility for an area of the organization in which expert power is required, and responsibility for an area in which there are a large proportion of the organization's employees. Although these are not strict requirements, possession of these areas makes the game easier to win.

> Those who desire a city to achieve great empire must endeavor by all possible means to make her populous; for without an abundance of inhabitants it is impossible ever to make a city powerful. This may be done in two ways; either by attracting population by the advantages offered, or by compulsion. The first is to make it easy and secure for strangers to come and establish themselves there, and the second is to destroy the neighboring cities, and to compel their inhabitants to come and dwell in yours.
>
> (*The Discourses*: 235)

As in all other aspects of being a good leader, you build an empire not for personal prestige but for the benefit it brings the organization. Your empire is necessary for the organization to be successful. And when building an empire, you must also amass the necessary power to go with it. Indeed, many a leader has acquired an empire he could not control, and subsequently lost all that he had gained.

> [F]or one may well extend one's dominion without increasing one's power, but the acquisition of dominion without power is sure to bring with it ruin. Whoever impoverishes himself by war acquires no power, even though he be victorious, for his conquests cost him more than they are worth . . . [with the desire of aggrandizement, must be the] knowledge of the proper means [of obtaining it].
>
> (*The Discourses*: 281)

THE BUDGET GAME

Empires are also built by having more machines, more people, and the budget that goes with supporting those things. It is important in the control of your empire that you acquire the largest possible budget. This is partly accomplished by playing the budget game. In this game you request a larger budget (money or resources) than you need, knowing in advance that your request will be trimmed. This is aided by including spurious projects in your budget that can be sacrificed without causing detriment to your empire.

But don't just rely on this one budget tactic. You should use an assortment of tactics in playing the budget game. Develop a series of arguments that support a large budget, and suppress the arguments of those who are in opposition to your budget request. (Mintzberg: 1983) If necessary, distort the truth about the real needs of your unit. Increase your needs for staffing and the projected cost of operating your unit. Never turn in funds from a previous period's budget. When the budget year is drawing to a close and you have excess funds, spend, spend, spend—regardless of real need. This is true because most organizations make a critical mistake in automatically subtracting excess funds of a previous period from the next period's budget. This tendency reinforces the manager's tendency to spend, spend, spend.

The budget game is important in building an empire because it is always true that those with more resources can bring about changes more effectively and faster than those with less.

[An organization] is either well armed . . . or it is not well armed . . . In the latter case you must keep the enemy at a distance; for as your strength consists in your money, and not in soldiers, you are lost whenever you are prevented from availing of your financial resources, and nothing interferes so much with that as war within your own territory.

(The Discourses: 257)

Princes [should] store and strengthen the towns in which they dwell, and take no heed of the country outside. For whoever has thoroughly fortified his town, and put himself on such a footing with his subjects . . . will never be attacked without [the attacker being cautious]; for men are always averse to enterprises in which they foresee difficulty, and it is impossible not to foresee difficulty in attacking a Prince whose town is strongly fortified and who is not hated by his subjects.

(The Prince: 74)

A Prince, therefore who has a strong city, and does not make himself hated, cannot be attacked, or should he be so, his assailant will come badly off.

(The Prince: 75)

Capital Budgets

When preparing a capital budget you must vary the general tactic of requesting more and project the cost on the down side—request less than is actually needed—and overstate the benefits. This will aid in gaining project approval, and in time you will be able to modify your request. The more technical or specialized a capital project, the easier it is to develop fuzzy figures. If you have limits to the spending you can approve, break up the cost of a capital item into smaller units so that they fit within your approval limits.

You must always be aware that the reason the organization withholds your request for an adequate budget is that there is someone else in the organization who is playing his own budget game. Other managers—often your opponents—recognize that when you have the resources necessary to accomplish your objectives, you will receive more power than they do.

Defenses against the Budget Game

When you are highly placed in the organization, and responsible for the overall performance of the organization, or when the enterprise belongs to you, whether in the form of a proprietorship, partnership, or corporation, it is necessary to remember that others in submitting requests to you for money may be playing the budget game.

The best method in controlling the actions of others who play this game is to base their budgets not on estimates alone but on a relationship between performance and total budget. Allow a portion of their budget to be approved only if they meet specific performance objectives. Do not punish them from one budget period to the next for having leftover funds. In other words, rewrite the rules to your advantage, but not to their detriment. This assist in limiting the overall expenses of the organization is very important if you are to expand your empire by acquiring other organizations, either internally or externally.

The object of those who make war, either from choice or ambition, is to conquer and to maintain their conquests, and to do this in such a manner as to enrich themselves and not to impoverish the conquered country. To do this, then, the conqueror should take care not to spend too much, and in all things mainly to look to the public benefit; and therefore he should imitate the manner and conduct of the Romans, which was first of all to "make the war short and sharp."

(*The Discourses*: 243)

Building an empire is not easy, but building it is not as difficult as directing its course.

[T]hose who had the direction of the government of states would have been better able to point out the means of aggrandizement, or the means of preservation. [They would know the policies to follow.]

(*The Discourses*: 279)

An empire once established is held by constructive uses of the powers that have been previously discussed. And a method of ensuring that a division is kept viable and always an important part of the organization, is to include in its purposes the creation, distribution, and storage of information.

THE EXPERT/INFORMATION GAME

This game is based upon a player having knowledge of what is going on in the organization, or having expert information about how to solve organizational problems, that other players do not possess. The more information of this kind you gain that is valuable to the organization, the more successful you will be in building an empire or maintaining your position in someone else's empire.

Information is the one product in which all organizations deal—it is in fact every organization's most important product—and the one service that every subunit in the organization should treat as a valuable commodity. Information is created by the production of reports, graphs, charts, or other devices that show either how the company is doing or what it should be doing. While much of this information is valuable, it is a weakness of most organizations that they waste resources in developing too much information. Conversely, when playing the information game, this is a weakness that you should capitalize on. Your organization should create all the information it can—needed or not.

However, if you are the owner or the chief executive officer of an organization, you should be on the watch for people who spend too much of their time creating an abundance of information. They may merely be playing the game, and their activities should be monitored.

Other problems that may result from the information game are an organization's desire to keep all the information it creates or an inability on its part to crystallize information into a concise format. This desire helps others play the game to their advantage and to the disadvantage of the organization. Many an empire has been built based on this perceived need to know everything.

When the empire is yours, and you are trying to control the game-playing of others, you should decide what information is important, how much it costs to store, and how much you lose by not having the information.

For example, you might determine that it cost $100,000 annually to keep all the information necessary to make a decision about a particular course of action. The cost of making the wrong decision may only be $25,000 annually. Therefore, the wise decision would be to choose not to store all the information, but to take the calculated risk of not having the information if needed. The cost attributable to not having information when it is needed is called instore cost. And if it is less than the cost of storage, then it is better to expend it.

Types of Information

A major tactic in the information game is not only to maintain specialized information, but to control the flow of organizational information that other people want or need.

[N]othing was more necessary and useful for a general than to know the intentions and projects of the enemy. And the more difficult it is to acquire such knowledge, the more praise he deserves who succeeds in [predicting] it correctly.

(The Discourses: 373)

For it has happened many a time that, when a battle has lasted until nightfall, the victor thinks himself beaten, and the defeated imagines himself to have been victorious. Such errors have caused men to resolve upon acts that proved their ruin.

(The Discourses: 373)

However, controlling information can result in keeping the wrong kind of information, and the consequences of this can be as disastrous as not having any information at all. The right information, which is called imperial information, is that which is needed to make executive decisions. This information is valuable not only in building your empire, but also in maintaining it.

Expert Information

Another type of information, expert information, is that information which you acquire through investment of time in various educational pursuits or by maintaining relationships that allow you special access to information.

[T]here are three scales of intelligence, one which understands by itself, a second which understands what is shown it by others, and a third which understands neither by itself nor on the showing of others, the first of which is most excellent, the second good, but the third worthless.

(The Prince: 172)

A tactic used by some in the information game is to attempt to win by pretending to have valuable information, or to have expert knowledge, when in fact they do not. This is dangerous and will be shunned by those who are wise; nevertheless, it is often practiced by those who label themselves experts or technocrats. And it is a method that many in the organization will use in their attempts to gain power.

Defenses against the Information/Expert Game

You can protect yourself against those who attempt to use Expert Information to your disadvantage by maintaining a staff in which no one person can control the destiny of the organization or stop work from proceeding.

[T]he institutions of a [organization] never should place it in the power of a few to interrupt all the important business of the [organization].

(The Discourses: 200)

It should be your goal to develop a staff with specialized knowledge spread among the many. On this staff, the attribute of being a generalist is considered valuable. This is not to say that you seek staff members who know only a little about a lot, but rather staff members who know a lot about a lot.

As an alternative, if you have acquired a staff that does not have generalized capabilities or if you are unable to produce such a staff, you should assure that there are written procedures (job duties) for what each of your staff members do, and how they do it. This will enable you to continue the daily operations of the organization should a specialist not be available. And it lessens the specialist's ability to threaten the organization with the loss of his knowledge.

A tactic of those who would use their expert power against you is to keep all the knowledge of what they do to themselves, keeping even the simplest duties a secret from others. You can circumvent this by having knowledge of where you can hire people on a temporary basis to perform the necessary organizational work that these experts perform. And occasionally it is wise to have these temporary employees assist your current staff in performing their duties. This sends them the message that the organization would not fold without them. This is one exception to the need to avoid reliance on temporary workers, which I will discuss in a later chapter.

Information control is critical to empire building, and by playing the game properly it will enable you to acquire and maintain power in the organization, thereby assisting you in your quest for success.

THE RESULTS OF GAMES

If you are to be a responsible manager, it is important to recognize that all games played by members of an organization can have repercussions far beyond the mere event of winning or losing. Game results affect players, their friends and families, and often even strangers. A wise and good manager cares and worries about the feelings of others in the organization. He is often in pain himself when it is necessary to cause hurt to others.

So before playing power games it is your responsibility to know your opponents, and know their motives for playing. Indeed, it is a wise manager who knows his friends and their reasons for being friendly. And it is also in your interest to know your enemies and give them the respect they deserve.

For of men it may generally be affirmed that they are thankless, fickle, false, studious to avoid danger, greedy of gain, devoted to you while you confer benefits upon them, and ready . . . while the need is remote, to shed their blood, and sacrifice their property, their lives, and their children for you; but when it comes near they turn against you.

(*The Prince*: 120)

6
Maintaining an Empire

Envy may be extinguished in two ways, either by some extraordinary and difficult occasion when everyone fears his own destruction, and therefore lays aside all ambition, and eagerly obeys any one whom he supposes capable of averting the danger by his virtues and talents . . . [or] when either violence or a natural death carries off those of your rivals who on seeing you acquire such reputation and greatness cannot patiently bear your being more distinguished than themselves.

(*The Discourses*: 397–98)

In maintaining an empire you must keep uppermost in your mind that neither emperors or empires last forever. The game in which others attempt to take your empire, or you attempt to take the empires of others, is called the rivals game. You should remember that regardless of how hard you work to build and maintain your empire, someone else will be trying to destroy it. And this is true not only in a large multinational organization where multi-empires abound, but also in smaller organizations.

The threat against your empire may be by an internal opponent within the same organization, a subordinate, a superior, or a peer, or it may be from an external opponent, another company, irate customers, former employees, or the government.

It is not important whether foes even consciously know that they are trying to destroy what you have—often they will not. They may be innocent in their motives, but deadly in their actions.

THE RIVALS GAME

There are several different methods of playing the rivals game. The game may consist of line managers against staff specialists, or of line managers against other line managers. It may be one against one or one against many.

When the game is one of line managers versus staff, it is usually a result of one of the players attempting to gain decision-making authority over another. A staff specialist might make an attempt to exert influence over higher-ranked decision makers, in an attempt to persuade them that he is correct in his evaluation of a situation and his opponent is not. The play usually begins when the staff specialist attempts to instigate changes in an operating unit. In these cases the changes are almost always to the detriment of the operating manager's empire. Thus, his ability to lead the organization is threatened. (Mintzberg: 1983) The staff person usually uses his position as an expert—gamma power—to attack the operating manager. This is especially true when gamma power makes up most of the specialist's total power. Since such persons generally have access to other managers, including the superiors of those against whom they are playing the game, they play by making misleading statements about the manager or the manager's unit.

Managers who have staff managers reporting to them should be aware of this tendency and accept all reports from them with caution until such time as a staff person has proved both reliability and loyalty.

In order for line managers to compete effectively in these games, they must avoid becoming one-sided specialists. If they do not, they have failed to gain an advantage over the specialist. A wise manager should keep abreast of what is happening not only in the organization, but also within his industry, and be knowledgeable about world events. The more you know, the better you will be at winning games. For it is by acquiring more knowledge that you will be able to acquire promotions and ultimately larger empires.

Fortune changes and men stand fixed in their old ways, they are [successful] so long as there is congruity between them, and [unsuccessful] when there is not.
(*The Prince:* 189)

When the game is one of line managers, or groups of line managers, against each other, it is an attempt by one manager or group to capture either some of their opponents or else their empire, in order to increase their own empire. The play can begin by one manager attempting to acquire resources, staff, or equipment from another manager, perhaps on a temporary basis, and evolve into the manager taking over the responsibilities of his opponent. This enables the one who is successful to be in a better position to play the budget game and increase his empire.

You can never be sure who your opponents are in the rivals game. Threats can even come from those you have previously built alliances with, if you have failed to assure that your alliances are ones in which you maintain control.

Once the rivals game has begun, especially when it is one in which a line manager is opposing another line manager, the players can ill afford to turn back. Because the purpose of the game is for there to be only one winner, by quitting you become a de facto loser. There are no silver or bronze medals awarded. During the game there may be temporary realignments, or if there are several players, there may be modifications of policies and procedures. If key persons in the organization see that the game is hurting the entire organization, they may insert themselves in the game as referees and transfer some of the players in order to bring the game under control.

How the Rivals Game Begins

The rivals game is usually the result of one player wanting a change and the other favoring the status quo or wanting a different change. It can be based upon differences in the players' management philosophy, or it can result from a personality conflict between the players.

There is no more delicate matter to take in hand, nor more dangerous to conduct, nor more doubtful in its success, than to [be] a leader in the introduction of changes. For he who innovates will have for enemies all those who are well off under the old order of things, and only lukewarm supporters in those who might be better off under the new. This lukewarm temper arises partly through fear of adversaries who have the laws on their side, and partly from the incredulity of mankind, who will never accept anything new, until they have seen it proved by the event.

(*The Prince*: 34–35)

While playing the rivals game you can simultaneously play some of the other games in order to help your position.

Anyone Can Start a War—Few Can End One

The rivals game can be waged on the open battlefield or else under cover of darkness. When it is played in darkness some players may not even know they are in the game until they lose. If you choose to play on the open field, it is better not to enter play until not only is your empire large enough, but your staff is both loyal and experienced.

Everyone may begin a war at his pleasure, but cannot so finish it. A prince, therefore, before engaging in any enterprise should well measure his strength, and govern himself accordingly; and he must be very careful not to deceive himself in the estimate of his strength.

(*The Discourses*: 251)

CONSPIRATORIAL GAMES

When a player or group of players plots to involve someone else in one of their games, they become conspiratorial. These are in reality subversive management actions, as opposed to management game playing.

There is, then, no greater misfortune for a prince than that a conspiracy should be formed against him; for it either causes his death, or it dishonors him. If the conspiracy succeeds, he dies; if it be discovered, and he punishes the conspirators with death, it will always be believed that it was an invention of the prince to satisfy his cruelty and avarice with the blood and possessions of those whom he had put to death.

(*The Discourses*: 347)

THE UNKNOWN SECRET TACTIC

One tactic in reacting to an opponent in any of the games is to employ the unknown secret tactic. This is used off the battlefield, although the ploy becomes a part of the game.

[C]alumnies require neither witnesses, nor confrontings, nor any particulars to prove them, so that every citizen may be calumniated by another [while] accusations cannot be lodged against any one without being accompanied by positive proofs and circumstances that demonstrate the truth of the accusation.

(*The Discourses*: 118)

It is a truth that everyone has done something that they would rather others did not know. And it is to your advantage to find out what that something is. If that is not practical, then act as if you know. It is not necessary to tell others what you know, and if you do tell, it can be to your detriment; because by telling, you lose the trust of others. However, if a game is not going well, it can prove beneficial to create a situation in which someone else starts a negative rumor about the person. This is the unknown secret.

And [among] the other means which ambitious citizens frequently employed to achieve power was this practice of calumniating, which, when employed against one noble citizen who opposed the ambitious projects of another, did much for the latter.

(*The Discourses*: 119)

But at all cost avoid the reputation of being a rumor monger; it is not befitting to a manager's position and will not help in maintaining an empire.

CHALLENGING THE MANAGER

A variation of the rivals game is either played by nonmanagers against other nonmanagers or by nonmanagers against managers. In the former, the exact nature depends on the position of the players in the organization, while in the latter the nonmanager makes a direct challenge to the manager's authority, especially if the manager's total power is by the challenger perceived to be low.

[M]en, thinking to better their condition, are always ready to change masters, and in this expectation will take up arms against any ruler; wherein they deceive themselves, and find afterwards by experience that they are worse off than before.

(*The Prince*: 4)

Those who have been present at any deliberative assemblies of men will have observed how erroneous their opinions often are; and in fact, unless they are directed by superior men, they are apt to be contrary to all reason. But as superior men in corrupt republics (especially in periods of peace and quiet) are generally hated, either from jealousy or the ambition of others, it follows that the preference is given to what common error approves, or to what is suggested by men who are more desirous of pleasing the masses than of promoting the general good.

(*The Discourses*: 286)

The purpose of the challenge is to neutralize the authority of the manager in order either to cause a transfer of the manager to a different department or to cause the manager to be removed from the organization. The game can be the result of a manager becoming arrogant in his attitude and being disliked by his employees. However, it is most often played by employees who find their jobs threatened through their incompetence or who are organizational malcontents because of their perception of what the organization has done to them. They turn their own incompetence or dissatisfaction into hatred. In these cases the manager should do all he can to remove them from the game board.

[B]y an utter disregard of his dignity, in frequently descending into the arena to fight with the gladiators, and by other base acts wholly unworthy of the Imperial station, he became contemptible in the eyes of the [soldiers]; and being on the one hand hated, on the other despised, was at last conspired against and murdered.

(*The Prince*: 147–48)

[M]en should honor the past and obey the present; and [while] they should desire good princes, they should bear with those they have, such as they are; and surely whoever acts otherwise will generally involve himself and his [organization] in ruin.

(The Discourses: 329)

THE CANDIDATES GAME

This game is played to cause organizational change. It is played by a player or group of players selecting a candidate to represent their cause.

[T]he people are guided in their choice either by what is said of a man by the public voice and fame, even if by his open acts he appears different, or by the preconceptions or opinion which they may have formed of him themselves.

(The Discourses: 406)

The candidate, if successful, will support them in their play of other games. The candidate can be used as both a sponsor and an ally. They can assist in supporting budget requests when he is playing the budget game; and they will also prove useful to him in winning the rivals game. Your candidate, if he wins, can become the cornerstone in building your empire.

At times it might be practical to support several different candidates, thereby increasing your chances of a winner. However it is usually best, especially if the candidates are in opposition to each other, to side with only one. Become their ally. You win this game when others in the organization see your candidate as right, or in cases where your candidate competes for high position and wins.

THE YOUNG TURKS GAME

The Young Turks game is one of high stakes—a game not to effect simple change, as in the previous games, but to restructure the very foundations of the organization. The entire organization is the game board, and the Young Turks want to shake everyone's empire. The players are generally highly placed senior executives—power players; their goal is to make fundamental changes in the organization. Either they may be trying to change the basic management philosophy of the organization, or they may have determined that the most effective way of winning is to replace the chief executive officer.

The Young Turks generally have access to key decision makers who can support their purposes and effect the change they desire. It is always to your advantage when playing as a Young Turk to keep the group as small as possible and the list of players and their purpose secret—until the time of the coup.

In this game the battle can become fierce and the competition deadly, because the primary objective is not to overthrow the management system, as in some of the other games, but to overthrow the creators of the system and take their place.

If you are a chief executive officer and the game is being played against you, there are two countermoves you can make. The first is to challenge the players openly and seek to expel them, destroying them and their game board.

Whoever, therefore, attacks the Turk must reckon on finding a united people, and must trust rather to his own strength than to divisions on the other side. But were his adversary once so crushed and routed in the field . . . no cause for anxiety would remain, except in the family [and friends] of the Prince; which being extirpated, there would be none else to fear; for since all beside are without credit with the people, the invader, as before his victory he had nothing to hope from them, so after it has nothing to dread.

(*The Prince*: 24–25)

The second is to accommodate their challenge, but only to a degree. You can make some of the changes they desire, as well as give them the authority to pursue their activities within the framework of your rules.

You should always keep in mind the dangers of this game. When players see they are losing the game and the probable result will be their expulsion from the organization, as their final gambit they may choose to turn the insurgency into a revolution. In this end game all the stops are pulled out. And the results of this all-or-nothing play becomes at the very least zero-sum, in which there are an equal number of winners and losers, and very possibly null-sum, in which there are no winners, only losers.

THE WHISTLE-BLOWING GAME

A final game, which can be played by both managers and nonmanagers, is the whistle-blowing game. This is as much an attempt at an organizational coup de grace as it is a game in itself.

[D]eaths . . . which are the result of a deliberate and fixed resolve, cannot be escaped by Princes, since any one who disregards his own life can effect them. A Prince, however, needs the less to fear them as they are seldom attempted.

(*The Prince*: 146)

The whistle-blowing game can be played by anyone and is often the end game of a manager who finds that he is losing one of the other games. It is filled with danger and often ruins the careers of both players and opponents. It can be directed either against the organization, or an individual in the organization, usually your opponent. It is generally based upon information the player has that can cause damage to the opponent—about tax evasion, breach of contract, or other illegal or questionable acts. Or it can merely be pretended knowledge—red herrings, to cause temporary problems for the opponent.

Well-known variations of this game are played by competitors blowing the whistle on other competitors to external agencies—government agencies, news organizations, inspection agencies. Or by spouses (usually ex-spouses) who blow the whistle on their husbands or wives to competitors or to government agencies. This is an extremely popular game for government enforcement agencies because of the valuable information they gain, and they often seek out players of this game to assist them in investigations.

[H]ow vain the faith and promises of men who are exiles from their own country. As to their faith, we have to bear in mind that, whenever they can return to their country by other means than your assistance, they will abandon you and look to the other means, regardless of their promises to you.

(*The Discourses*: 313)

The outcome of the whistle-blowing game is usually zero-sum, with the winner more often than not the government. But it can also be a null-sum game, in which everyone loses.

Whistle-blowing games can be hazardous to all players, and this is especially true when the person who had the whistle blown on him knows who blew the whistle. Revenge often sounds sweet to the ears of such a person and has often ended in real death, not just corporate death. Therefore, it is a wise strategy for the whistle blowers to keep their actions secret. However, most whistle blowers do not feel redeemed unless the target knows of their actions. When playing this game it is best to keep your victory (if there is one) to yourself.

From this we plainly see the folly and imprudence of demanding a thing, and saying beforehand that it is intended to be used for evil; and that one should never show one's intentions, but endeavor to obtain one's desires anyhow. For it is enough to ask a man to give up his arms, without telling him that you intend killing him with them; after you have the arms in hand, then you can do your will with them.

(*The Discourses*: 190)

GAMES OF INSURRECTION

Before playing games of insurrection, or in countering the actions of those who play these games, you should assure yourself that you can live not only with the consequences of losing but the consequences of winning. The winner of an insurrection usually becomes the target for another group of rioters.

Managers should note well the advice of Frederick Engels when playing games that deal in a form of insurrection—such as Games of Insurgency and The Young Turks Game—or in countering the actions of those who play games of insurrection:

Now, insurrection is an art quite as much as war or any other, and subject to certain rules of proceeding, which, when neglected, will produce the ruin of the party neglecting them. Those rules, logical deductions from the nature of the parties and the circumstances one has to deal with in such case, are so plain and simple. . . . Firstly, never play with insurrection unless you are fully prepared to face the consequences of your play. Insurrection is a calculus with very indefinite magnitudes the value of which may change every day; the forces against you have all the advantage of organization, discipline, and habitual authority; unless you bring strong odds against them you are defeated and ruined. Secondly, the insurrectionary career once entered upon, act with the greatest determination, and on the offensive. The defensive is the death of every armed rising; it is lost before it measures itself with its enemies. Surprise your antagonists while their forces are scattering, prepare new successes, however small, but daily; keep up the moral ascendancy which the first successful rising has given to you; rally those vacillating elements to you which always follow the strongest impulse, and which always look out for the safer side; force your enemies to retreat before they can collect their strength against you.

(Engels, 1933, p. 100)

BE PREPARED

A wise manager will avoid an abundance of game playing but will be a talented player when called upon to compete. This can only be done through preparation. If a manager is prepared, when an opponent challenges him on the organizational field of battle, he will have the victory.

[T]o organize for war as to be ever prepared for it.

(*The Discourses*: 371)

For among other causes of misfortune which your not being armed brings upon you, it makes you despised, and this is one of those reproaches against which . . . a Prince ought most carefully to guard. Between an armed and an unarmed man no proportion holds, and it is contrary to reason to expect that the armed man should willingly obey him who is unarmed, or that the unarmed man should stand secure among armed followers.

(*The Prince:* 104)

7

Foundations of an Empire

[H]e who does not lay his foundations at first, may, if he be [of great ability], succeed in laying them afterwards, though with inconvenience to the builder and risk to the building.

(The Prince: 41)

Acquiring and maintaining an empire can be through fortune, through the assistance of allies or through your own individual actions. However, your own efforts are always strengthened through the assistance of allies. But regardless of the method used, it is necessary to prepare yourself to be capable of managing the empire that you create or acquire.

This is done through study, experience, and development of a positive attitude. In general the empire-builder should study business, economics, management, history, and liberal arts. And his education should consist of both formal and informal educational pursuits.

A Prince, therefore, should have no care or thought but for war, and for the discipline and training it requires, and should apply himself exclusively to this as his peculiar province; for this is the sole art looked for in one who commands, and is of such efficacy that it not merely maintains those who are born Princes, but often enables men to rise to that eminence from a private station.

(The Prince: 103)

EXPERIENCE COUNTS

Experience is gained not only by the passing of time, but also by spending your time engaged in a wide variety of business and organizational activities.

Certain events also easily mislead men who have not a great deal of experience, for they have in them so much that resembles truth that men easily persuade themselves that they are correct in the judgment they have formed upon the subject.

(*The Discourses*: 286–87)

HAVE A POSITIVE ATTITUDE

A positive attitude is gained by developing an adequate amount of self-confidence. And this is done by participating in activities in which you can achieve victory or success such as competitive games or sports. Do not wait for problems to arise before you become concerned about your ability to accomplish difficult tasks. Every little breeze of improvement increases your chances of being victorious in whatever you do.

A Prince, therefore, ought never to allow his attention to be diverted from warlike pursuits, and should occupy himself [with them] even more in peace than in war. This he can do in two ways, [by action and study].

(*The Prince*: 104–5)

BE GRACIOUS IN DEFEAT

And while winning and being victorious is important, it is also necessary that you develop an ability to be gracious in the defeats you encounter. This does not imply that you feel good about losing; but it does mean that you express a positive attitude to your opponents whether you win or lose. This not only positions you to play the game again, but it assures that you will have worthy opponents. No one likes a loser who is not generous in defeat.

[A] general may acquire glory in any action; in victory it follows as a matter of course, and in defeat it may be acquired, either by showing that it was not due to any fault of his, or by promptly doing some act that neutralizes the effects of the defeat.

(*The Discourses*: 422)

[No] army . . . is absolutely invincible . . . [You must not] calculate the uselessness . . . from the loss of one battle, but are rather to believe that having miscarried once, they will be more cautious afterwards, and do something (as occasion offers) to expiate their disgrace.

(*The Art of War*: 444)

ESTABLISH GOALS AND OBJECTIVES

Another important ingredient in the prescription for victory is having goals and objectives for whatever it is you want to accomplish. And to be valuable these goals must be measurable both in terms of what you wish to achieve and when you wish to achieve it. Goals without guideposts are useless. And after you have set your goals you must make periodic evaluations of whether or not you are achieving them. If you do not know where it is you are going, you will never know when you get there, and if you don't have a time to be there, you will not know whether you are late.

[E]very man's [goal] is to put himself into a condition of giving the Enemy battle, and fighting him fairly in the field.

(*The Art of War*: 442)

If you are achieving your goals with little effort, then you should adjust them upwards and become more demanding of yourself. If you are not achieving your goals, then you should figure out why. If the reason for nonachievement is that they were unrealistically high; then they should be adjusted downward. If the deficiency lies in your failure to take the necessary actions to achieve them, then you should immediately correct your conduct.

Men who are born in a republic, therefore, should . . . strive to distinguish themselves by some remarkable action.

(*The Discourses*: 407)

SIMPLE SOLUTIONS MARK THE ROAD TO FAILURE

In order to develop a positive attitude, gain self-confidence, and achieve your goals, it is important to be comfortable with yourself. Indeed, if you are not comfortable with yourself, how can you expect others to have confidence in you? You should learn to spend time with yourself, relaxing and visualizing yourself in the state you want to achieve. However, be warned that, by themselves, neither visualizing nor relaxing will help you obtain your goals, nor will the mere recital of mantras or words of encouragement. Unless they are coupled with psychological change and thoughtful study, these are mere formulas of foolishness. And many managers become victims of the ''quick fix,'' wanting the easy solution, one without effort. They spend their time and money foolishly pursuing vain promises of success.

To use the principles of relaxation and visualizing, it is necessary to develop the ability to engage your total mind in the process. And this is only done through practice. Your goals must penetrate your psyche. But at the same time, you must be engaged in activities that will make you capable of achieving those objectives. By itself, visualizing will not make you more knowledgeable; the necessary reading and studying are also required. You will never dream yourself to success. If you do only this, you will wake up and find yourself further behind than you were when you began your dream. There is no magic formula for achieving power and success—it takes both mental and physical effort.

As to the mental training, . . . a Prince should read histories, and in these should note the actions of great men, observe how they conducted themselves in their wars, and examine the causes of their victories and defeats, so as to avoid the latter and imitate them in the former. And above all, he should, as many great men of past ages have done, assume for his model some one person who before his time has been renowned and celebrated, whose deeds and achievements he should constantly keep in mind.

(The Prince: 107)

HARD WORK IS A NECESSITY

Those who strive to reach the highest levels of management cannot just work the standard work week. In order to keep ahead of others you must be constantly striving to achieve your goals, and persevere no matter what obstacles you encounter. Your strategies for keeping ahead might include working nights or weekends, taking educational courses away from your office, or carrying out an individual program of reading and study in various subjects. You must always be preparing yourself to be worthy of the goals you are seeking.

That which is beneficial to you, is [harmful] to your Enemy, and that which is beneficial to him, is [harmful] to you.

(The Art of War: 519)

Nature produces few persons strong; but [effort and training] makes many.

(The Art of War: 519)

Order and discipline [does more in war] than [enthusiasm].

(The Art of War: 519)

SEIZE THE MOMENT

The cardinal question that is often asked by managers is: Does the moment make the person, or the person make the moment? It is neither, but rather the interaction of the two. Being prepared for the moment creates successes. You must overcome the moment when necessary, accommodate it when required, and always seize it for your advantage.

A wise Prince, therefore, should pursue such methods as these, never resting idle in times of peace, but strenuously seeking to turn them to account, so that he may derive strength from them in the hour of danger, and find himself ready should Fortune [change], to resist [it].

(The Prince: 108)

YOU CAN'T LEARN FROM EXPERIENCES YOU'RE NOT HAVING

A manager must constantly prepare himself for the moment of opportunity. And you can only prepare yourself through a variety of experiences. It is necessary to have as many diverse and valuable experiences as you can. And for the thoughtful, creative manager, learning experiences are numerous. While it is not possible to predict what you will learn from an experience, because the lesson learned or idea gained is a result of your uniqueness, and your situation at the time of the experience, it is important to have experiences. And because your perspective changes the lesson you learn, have each experience more than once. I could list a thousand experiences you should have but space does not permit this, so I will just list a few in order to stimulate your thinking about experiences you should have: receiving poor customer service at McDonald's, taking a cruise in the Caribbean, returning a purchase at a retail store, dealing with a major manufacturer regarding a service policy, taking a ride on the Matterhorn at Disneyland, sitting through a bumpy landing on an airplane, strolling in the rain, or visiting a trade show. You can learn from almost anything, but you can not learn from experiences that you are not having. So be sure to experience life, and learn from those experiences.

8

The Strengths of Empires

[T]hose [who can] stand alone [are those] who, with the men or money at their disposal, can get together an army fit to take the field against any assailant; and, conversely, [those] . . . in constant need of help [are those] who cannot face their enemies in the open field, but are obliged to retire behind their walls, and [be on the defensive].

(The Prince: 73)

In organizations, strength and power is acquired through numbers. If an organization is to survive and grow, it must be able to enter new markets and develop new products. And this is only done through the cooperation of a large number of motivated, hardworking employees and a large bank account. If you are to acquire other organizations through takeovers, you must have money to buy when the opportunity is right. And if you are to successfully provide good service to your customers, you must have employees who care for you and your organization.

If you belong to an organization where there are numerous departments and divisions, often your position depends on the number of employees assigned to your division and their merits. And these employees are especially necessary when competing in games for power. Resistance from others who are trying to acquire your empire can be overcome by having a larger organization than they have. And you can make up for differences in the size of staffs by assuring that your staff is more motivated than theirs.

[I]t is not sufficient . . . to understand how to manage [an organization]; but you must first know how to make and prepare it, and then how to [manage] and conduct it.

(*The Art of War*: 522)

If your employees do not maintain a high level of motivation, then you and your organization will suffer. And in order to maintain a high level of motivation, it is necessary to create an environment in which your employees are at ease and happy. When this is true, they are more willing to come to your defense should the occasion arise.

Another measure of strength in large corporate organizations is the number of shares of stock you hold, or the number of proxies you have, before organizational battles or realignments take place.

In the case of corporate raiders, in most instances a larger number of shares of stock can overcome the strength of having numerous employees.

OVERCOMING THE RAIDER

However, although this is rare, a well-organized company can overcome the strength of a corporate raider, if it is prepared to do mortal battle. For example, an organization that is under siege by a raider can employ a system of strikes, boycotts, and lockouts in order to drive the price of the stock to near ruin. If these actions be deemed illegal because of existing government rules and regulations, then its managers must accomplish the same objectives through creative artifice and sophistry. Their objective is to destroy the corporate raiders' financial position and convince them taking over their company is not worth the battle.

Thus the defense of fortified cities depends upon the arms and valor of the garrison, the same as in ancient times . . . But supposing . . . that you have chosen the highest ground . . . and that your entrenchments are good and sufficient, so that owing to your position and your other preparations the enemy does not venture to attack you, in that case he will resort to the same means as the ancients did when the adversary had placed himself in an impregnable position; that is, he will scour the country, plunder the towns and villages of your allies, and cut off your supplies of provisions, so that you will be forced to abandon your entrenchments and come to battle, where your artillery will avail you but little. . . . [R]emember that [the Roman] wars were aggressive and not defensive.

(*The Discourses*: 271)

WHY THE RAIDER WINS

But in almost all instances, the larger the organization the more disorganized it is. Because of faulty leadership, most participants look out for their own self-interest and will never sacrifice for the good of the many. In these cases, a determined raider who has strength in money and shares of stock can defeat any opponent.

If an organization is being attacked and it becomes obvious that management will be unable to buy or hold its position, then it is to its advantage, and yours, to accept the best terms possible. If managers have not prepared in advance for the onslaught, it is only wise for them to obtain terms that are beneficial to themselves.

Alexander found after four months of siege that the taking of the city would require more of his time and glory than most of his other conquests had done, and therefore resolved to try negotiations and to concede to the Tyrians all they themselves had asked. But the Tyrians on their part, having become elated, now refused to make terms, and killed the messengers whom Alexander had sent to them. This so enraged Alexander that he assaulted the city with such vigor that he captured and destroyed her, and made slaves of her men.

(*The Discourses*: 303)

PREPARING FOR THE TAKEOVER

You should not forget that raiders to your organization can be internal. It is a foolish manager and a foolish organization that has not prepared for an attempted takeover by a foe. Potential opponents should be discouraged from ever attempting a takeover action by the proactive actions of a manager. Do to them before they do to you. It is when managers become overconfident and fall victim to hubris that they become takeover targets. The best course of action for a manager or an organization is to acquire such a reputation that no one would ever attempt such an action.

[W]hen a prince or a people attain that degree of reputation that all the neighboring princes and peoples fear to attack him, none of them will ever venture to do it except under the force of necessity; so that it will be, as it were, at the option of that potent prince or people to make war upon such neighboring powers as may seem advantageous, [while] adroitly keeping the others quite. And this he can easily do, partly by the respect they have for his power, and partly because they are deceived by the means employed to keep them quiet.

(*The Discourses*: 228)

By being aware of the difficulties in protecting yourself and your organization, it is easier to maintain your empire through growth and, when necessary, to take over other organizations.

9
Why Managers Lose Empires

For men are more nearly touched by things present than by things past, and when they find themselves well off [in the present], enjoy their [peace] and seek [nothing else], [they] are ready to do their utmost in defense of the new Prince, if he [is not lacking] in other respects.

(*The Prince*: 179–80)

The things that I have mentioned, if wisely observed, enable a new manager to become established within an organization, just as if he had been there as long as older managers. And it is very important for a new manager to remember that his actions are more closely watched than those of established managers. If and when these actions are recognized to be fitting and proper, he wins employee and staff loyalty and commands respect. And if the successful actions of a new manager are observed and appreciated by established managers, he will become more secure and less likely to be a victim of organizational strife.

If the practices and principles discussed so far are followed by founders of organizations, these founders can become organizational legends, joining the ranks of leaders whose actions are worthy of imitation. However, not following these principles or following them with a malevolent attitude, in order to deceive and only accomplish your own self-interest, can prevent you from ever gaining an empire or cause you to lose any you gain. While abuse of the principles might lead to short-term successes, the foundations built upon those abuses are likely to crumble.

Managers have lost their empires for behaving in ways opposite to those recommended. They have failed to establish loyalties and friendships that would have enabled them to survive passing attacks. They have not prepared for the future and have not been able to change with the times. They have not been able to adapt to new methods or new technology.

They have failed to rid their organizations of malcontents and other undesirable workers. They have not avoided flattery and have been unwise in the appointment of their advisors. Their opponents saw their weaknesses and successfully attacked them, both overtly and covertly.

DEPEND ON YOURSELF AND YOUR ABILITY

[Those who] have lost their [empires should] blame not Fortune but their own ineptitude. For never having reflected in [peaceful] times that there might come a change (and it is human nature when the sea is calm not to think of storms), when adversity overtook them, they thought not of defense but only of escape, hoping that their people, disgusted with the insolence of the conqueror, would some day recall them. This course [of action] may be a good one to follow when all others fail, but it [is] the height of folly, trusting to it, [and neglecting all others]; since none would wish to fall on the chance that some one else will be found to lift him up. It may not happen [that anyone will help you], and should it happen, it gives you no security . . . and those modes of defense are alone good, certain, and lasting, which depend upon yourself and your own worth.

(The Prince: 181–82)

KNOW WHEN TO CHANGE YOUR
MIND AND CONDUCT

Managers have also lost their positions by not recognizing that as they change in management rank their new position requires a corresponding change in attitudes and opinions. Ideas they may have expressed in previous positions often are not valid or applicable after they have learned all the facts. Yet they fail to change.

It happened in several instances that these citizens did attain to the highest magistracy, and when they had risen to that place, and were enabled to see matters more closely, they discovered the real causes of the disorders, and the dangers that threatened the state, as well as the difficulty of remedying them. And seeing that the times, and not the men, caused the disorders, they promptly changed their opinions and actions, because the knowledge of things in particular had removed from their minds that delusion into which they had fallen by looking at things in general. So that those who at first had heard them speak [while] they were still private citizens, and afterwards saw them remain inactive when they had risen to the supreme magistracy, believed that this was caused, not by the real knowledge of things, but by their having been perverted and corrupted by the great. And as this happened with many, and repeatedly, it gave rise to a saying, ''That these people have one mind in the public places, and ''another mind in the palace.''

(*The Discourses*: 196)

10

Secretaries and Advisors

The choice of [advisors] is a matter of [great importance] to a Prince.
Whether they shall be good or [not] depends on his prudence, so that
the readiest conjecture we can form of his character and [competence],
is from seeing what sort of men he has about him. When they are
. . . capable and faithful, we . . . always account him wise, since he
has known to recognize their merit and to retain their [loyalty]. But
if they be [the opposite], we must . . . [think otherwise], since he had
already erred in making this selection.

(The Prince: 170)

It is a foolish manager who attempts to achieve excellence without
assistance from others. One of the most critical decisions you make as
a wise manager, or on your journey to becoming one, is who can you
trust to give you good advice; to watch out for your best interests, to tell
you the truth, to be your confidant. Good secretaries and good advisors
are few and far between, and it is indeed the privileged manager who
is able to acquire them.

What you are to do, you may [consult] with many; what you [decide] to do, communicate with few.

(The Art of War: 520)

SELECTING ADVISORS

The process of acquiring good advisors and secretaries is time consuming and full of assorted dangers. The interview process, no matter how detailed or how lengthy, is only a device in the selection process that allows you to select the ones who might be good. It takes time and experience in working with advisors and assistants before you are able to tell whether your decision in selecting them was correct.

Given the fact that many will want to be your advisors, you should be aware that most will say what they have to in order to get the job. Most people who interview for a position as your advisor will be concerned only with their self-interest, not yours. This is why the best advisors you can acquire are informal advisors who do not work directly for you in the organization, and sometimes don't even work for your organization.

SELECTING SECRETARIES

Your secretary is also a critical key to your success. A secretary you can trust will be of assistance in many ways. Not only does a secretary help you, in the day-to-day routine tasks, but the secretary becomes your eyes and ears within the organization. As this person gains experience in working with you, he or she becomes able to keep you informed of situations before they become problems, and often can defuse potential problems themselves.

The best gauge of whether your secretary or advisor is loyal is in his or her actions. These outweigh words as a measurement of loyalty.

As to how a Prince is to know his [advisor], this unerring rule may be laid down. When you see [an advisor] thinking more of himself than of you, and in all his actions seeking his own ends, that man can never be a good [advisor] or one that you can trust. For he who has the charge of the State committed to him, ought not to think of himself, but only of his Prince, to whose notice he should never bring what does not directly concern him.

(The Prince: 172–73)

Those managers who classify their secretaries or advisors as just regular staff or ordinary employees either do not have worthy individuals in the position or do not recognize their true value. If you treat your closest advisors in a cavalier manner, you will eventually lose their loyalty. They should be rewarded both for good performance and for loyalty. However, don't honor them just because they have the position. Honor them only if they have the talent to merit the position and perform in an acceptable manner. If they are disloyal to you, you should immediately rid yourself of them.

[T]o keep his [advisor] good, the Prince should be considerate of him, dignifying him, enriching him, binding him to himself by benefits, and sharing with him the honors as well as the burdens of the state, so that the abundant honors and wealth bestowed upon him may divert him from seeking these at other hands; while the great responsibilities . . . he is charged [with] may lead him to dread change, knowing that he cannot stand alone without his master's support. When Prince and [advisor] are upon this footing they can mutually trust one another, when the contrary is the case it will always fare ill with one or other of them.

(*The Prince*: 173)

USE CAUTION WITH ADVISORS

While treating advisors differently, you should exercise caution. Since they are closer to you than other employees or staff, they also have the potential to do you more harm.

A prince, then, who wishes to guard against conspiracies should fear those on whom he has heaped benefits quite as much, and even more, than those whom he has wronged; for the latter lack the convenient opportunities which the former have in abundance. The intention of both is the same, for the thirst of dominion is as great as that of revenge, and even greater. A prince, therefore, should never bestow so much authority upon his friends but that there should always be a certain distance between them and himself, and that there should always be something left for them to desire; otherwise they will almost invariably become victims of their own imprudence.

(*The Discourses*: 333)

[Plots by the many] have generally for their originators the great men of the state, or those on terms of familiar intercourse with the prince. None other, unless they are madmen, can engage in conspiracies; for men of low condition, who are not intimate with the prince, have no chance of success, not having the necessary conveniences for the execution of their plots.

(*The Discourses*: 332)

Good advisors and good secretaries can assist you in the management of your empire. To be good, they must be trained to perform to your expectations. The larger your organization, the more trust you must put in them, and the more critical the correct selection of them becomes.

If you have an organization that is located in different geographic regions, you should place a trusted advisor or a trusted secretary at each location in order to represent you and look out for your interests.

[A]ll Princedoms . . . have been governed . . . either by a sole Prince, all others being his servants, permitted . . . to assist in governing the kingdom as his [advisors]; or else by a Prince with his Barons.

(*The Prince*: 22–23)

You should never be unduly harsh with those who serve and assist you in important matters.

[He should] avoid doing grave wrong to any of those who serve him, or whom he has near him as officers of his Court.

(The Prince: 146–47)

However, this does not mean you should not use appropriate discipline with them. If advisors err, they should be removed from your counsel. Your advisors and secretaries are a reflection of you, and you will be partly judged by their behavior and their performance.

11

Auxiliary Workers

When David offered himself to Saul to go forth and fight Goliath the Philistine champion, Saul, to encourage him, armed him with his own armor, which David, [as] soon as he had put it on, rejected, saying that with these untried arms he could not prevail, and that he chose rather to meet his enemy with only his sling and sword. In a word, the armor of others is too wide, or too strait for us; it falls off us, it impedes us, or weights us down.

(The Prince: 99)

Management is getting things done through others. Leadership is the ability to get others to accomplish things at our behest, with quality results. Most of the time, you accomplish your objectives by utilizing staff that has been hired to perform specific tasks. However, at times there may be a need to subcontract with others, hire temporary staff, or rely on consultants. These become substitute or auxiliary employees, and although they can perform work to your advantage, their services should be limited and used with caution.

[A]uxiliary troops [are] such as a prince or republic send to your aid, but which are paid, and the commander of which is appointed by the prince or republic.

(The Discourses: 282)

SUBCONTRACTORS

Subcontracting is required when your organization is not capable of providing all of the materials or services it needs to operate. For example, you may contract with someone to provide your marketing services, as is sometimes done with manufacturing representatives. Or you may operate your information services department either with outside computer bureaus or by having another company come to your location and manage your computer facilities.

When you use subcontractors for needed services, you are putting your trust in the ability of others to rule your empire. You are depending upon the skills of others to have their personnel properly trained and motivated to perform tasks that are necessary for the success of your company. This can be done safely if the product or service they are providing is not critical to your operation and your organization can operate for a period of time without that product or service, should the persons you are depending on fail to provide it. But when you are relying on something that is critical to your organization, you jeopardize your position and power by depending on others.

[O]f all kinds of troops, auxiliaries are the most dangerous; for the prince or republic that calls them to their assistance has no control or authority whatever over them, as that remains entirely with him who sends them.

(The Discourses: 283)

It is therefore important that you organize in such a manner that you are always able to provide those services that are critical to your operation, and that you do not become overly dependent on outside sources.

A prince or republic, then, should adopt any other course rather than bring auxiliaries into their state for its defense, especially when their reliance is wholly upon them; for any treaty or convention with the enemy, however hard the conditions, will be less hard to bear than the danger from auxiliaries.

(The Discourses: 283)

TEMPORARY HELP

Temporary help is the help you use to handle work overloads or act as substitutes for your staff. The warnings given for depending on subcontractors are applicable to temporary workers. Temporary help will not be loyal to you in times of trouble, and they care little for the future of your organization or your well-being.

CONSULTANTS

Consultants are those whom you employ to give you advice on your organization and its method of operation. While sometimes necessary, they should be used with caution and moderation. At times they can be used to develop plans for which you do not want to become totally responsible. If those plans fail, you can then blame the failure on the consultants.

It is wise to be on watch for subordinate employees who attempt the same tactic, and hire or recommend the hiring of consultants to do a study or give advice on a task for which they are responsible. They often do this only to avoid responsibility, and in order to have someone to blame for the project's failure, or else they do it because they lack the skills to perform their jobs.

[Foreign soldiers] do more mischief than [your] own, for a popular Citizen may more easily corrupt and employ them as Instruments [to gain power].

(*The Art of War*: 444)

While this tactic is useful when you employ it, it is harmful to you when done by others.

Consultants, as with subcontractors and temporary workers, do not owe their loyalty to you and are only superficially interested in the maintenance of your position and power. Their interest is only present as long as your power can help them maintain their positions.

HAVE A FIRM FOUNDATION

All three types of workers have places in your organization and can be used to your advantage. However, before relying on their services, make sure that the foundations of your empire are firm.

Mercenaries and auxiliaries are at once useless and dangerous, and he who holds his State by means of mercenary troops can never be solidly or securely seated. For . . . [they are] disunited, ambitious, insubordinate, treacherous, insolent among friends . . . [and] cowardly before foes. . . . No sooner are you attacked than they fail you; so that in peace you are plundered by them, in war by your enemies.

(*The Prince*: 85)

As opposed to having too much reliance on auxiliary workers, it is wiser to develop some staff members who can perform multiple job functions. These staff persons are called generalists. If staffing problems develop within your organization, you can move them from location to location within the organization. This is especially helpful when other staff members are on vacation or otherwise unavailable to perform their jobs.

These generalists are usually more loyal to you than temporary help and have a vested interest in doing a good job.

[It is] a good thing to have Soldiers who have two strings to their bow [who can perform two tasks], and yield double advantage.

(The Art of War: 446)

A wise manager uses caution before employing these three types of auxiliary workers. They should be used as part of your war plan, but should not be expected to win the war.

[Managers and organizations] of modern times as have no national troops for defense or attack ought well to be ashamed of it.

(The Discourses: 149)

12
Motivating the Workers

[H]ow much more praise those Emperors merited who, after Rome became an empire, conformed to the laws like good princes, than those who took the opposite course. [They] did not require the Praetorian [guard] nor the multitudinous legions to defend them, because they were protected by their own good conduct, the good will of the people, and by the love of the Senate.

(The Discourses: 124)

A good leader finds strength and success by having highly motivated employees who are interested in his well-being and success and the successes and well-being of his organization.

When you begin a new organization or add to an existing one, you acquire these employees through good recruiting and selection. It is as important for a manager to recruit able people at the lowest position in the organization as it is to recruit qualified high-level managers. Indeed, an organization's strength is based on its weakest positions. Therefore, you should recruit employees not only who are well-trained, but also who are capable of being better trained.

Others have [had] not only to contend with and conquer the enemy, but [had] to [train] their Army; and these were . . . worthy of [great] praise. . . . [T]hey were able to do it [because they had subjects fit to receive such training.]

(The Art of War: 521)

A staff person can be a specialist or a generalist. A specialist is a person who knows a lot about one job, and is not very adept or flexible in performing other tasks. A generalist is a person who can perform a variety of jobs effectively. There is a place for both in an organization, and the prize worker is a specialist who has generalist capabilities.

EMPLOYEES' OPINIONS

Employees' opinions are important, both in building your organization and in gaining power within it. Their opinions should never be ignored because they are valuable in the development of the organization, and are often better than the opinions of subordinate managers. Employees have many experiences that managers do not have, and at times those experiences can be translated into good ideas. A good leader listens to all ideas and sifts the good from the bad. This listening does not mean that you should turn the decision-making process over to employees, but rather that you should be interested in their ideas and respect their opinions.

[N]o wise man should ever disregard the popular judgment upon particular matters, such as the distribution of honors and dignities; for in these things the people never deceive themselves, or, if they do, it is much less frequently than a small body would do, who had been especially charged with such distributions.
(The Discourses: 196)

The employees who work for an organization have characteristics that are the opposite of those of the auxiliary workers already discussed. If you have recruited your employees properly and trained and developed them with care, they will have some degree of loyalty and love. This is important to your success.

For armies that have no such affection towards him for whom they fight as to make them his partisans, will never have bravery enough to resist an enemy who has the least courage. And as this love and devotion can only be found in your own subjects, it is necessary for the purpose of holding a government, or to maintain a republic or kingdom, to have your army composed of your own subjects, as [has] been done by all those whose armies have achieved great successes.
(The Discourses: 188–89)

EMPLOYEES' AMBITIONS

In dealing with your employees, it is important to give them an opportunity to achieve some of their ambitions. If they do not have an opportunity to be themselves and to meet their own personal needs, they can become harmful to you.

The demands of a free people are rarely [destructive] to their liberty; they are generally inspired by oppressions, experienced or apprehended; and if their fears are ill founded, resort is had to public assemblies where the mere eloquence of a single good and respectable man will make them sensible of their error.

(The Discourses: 106)

You can assist your employees in achieving some of their ambitions by developing an employee organization and letting some of them be leaders in that organization, by promoting company sports teams in which employees can participate, and by allowing them to perform activities in which they can show they are better than either their fellow employees or employees of other companies. Especially effective are community fund-raising drives and sports events in which employees compete with employees of other companies.

QUALITY CIRCLES

Quality circles are group devices that bring together employees either from the same work group or from various work groups throughout the organization. While they are of little value by themselves because of their implied forced participation, they can do little harm if used in moderation. Judicious use of quality circles provides employees an outlet to vent their frustration. However, this tactic should be kept to a minimum because, too often, these circles become nonproductive. They give malcontents a stage to perform on and spread their discontent to other employees.

[E]very free state ought to afford the people the opportunity of giving vent, so to say, to their ambition; and above all those republics which on important occasions have to avail themselves of this very people.

(The Discourses: 106)

Whoever undertakes to govern a people . . . without making sure of those who are opposed to this new order of things establishes a government of very brief duration.

(The Discourses: 138–39)

MOTIVATING EMPLOYEES

In order to assure that you have employees who are motivated, it is best to recruit those who show some degree of self-motivation. However, just because you have employees who are self-motivated does not mean you can ignore the need to provide them with further motivation. You must provide them with a motive or motives for being loyal to you, for loving you and for loving the organization.

To make an army victorious in battle it is necessary to inspire them with confidence, so as to make them believe that the victory will be theirs under any circumstances.

(The Discourses: 404)

[T]hose Roman generals who made themselves beloved by their armies, and managed them with gentleness, obtain[ed] more success than those who made themselves feared in an extraordinary manner, unless the latter were gifted with uncommon virtues.

(The Discourses: 376)

This love and confidence is easier to develop whenever there is a spirit of organizational unity and loyalty. It is assisted by encouraging the staff to know each other on more than just a working basis. This is accomplished by using some of the group devices previously mentioned.

[T]o give an army such confidence they must be well armed and disciplined, and the men must know each other.

(The Discourses: 404)

It is also easier to motivate them when you are a positive example to them. The more successful you are, the better example you are.

I want you to follow my actions, and not merely my words; not my orders only, but the example of him who by his right arm has thrice achieved the consulate and the highest glory.

(The Discourses: 416)

Consider, then, under whose lead and auspices you are about to go into battle, and whether he to whom you are listening is merely a [pompous] orator, terrible only in words; or whether he is skilled in military matters and himself able to deal blows, to lead on the banners, and to combat in the thickest of the fight.

(The Discourses: 416)

In motivation, it is necessary for you, personally, to give them inspiring messages and to be consistent in doing this. And you should employ any other device that assists in developing their positive attitude; some of these devices are programs designed to assist them in furthering their education, liberal holiday and vacation programs, a financial bonus program linked to performance, and parties and dinners, which are savored for their convivial nature.

MONITOR ACTIONS OF EMPLOYEES

While doing all of these things to motivate employees, it is still necessary to monitor their actions. For you to be successful, it is necessary to develop the ability to see beyond what they are actually doing to why it is they are doing it. Many empires and leaders have been crushed because of the actions of employees who appeared to be loyal but who were instead opportunists who would market their services to the highest bidder. The deceit of employees of this type often takes the form of conspiracies. And conspiracies arise not only from the actions of other managers who are competing against you, but also from trusted staff and loyal employees.

[V]ery often actions that seem good on the surface, and which cannot reasonably be objected to, may become oppressive and highly dangerous to a republic unless they are corrected [in good time].

(The Discourses: 394)

[T]he institutions of the state should be so regulated that the influence of citizens shall be founded only upon such acts as are of benefit to the state, and not upon such as are injurious to the public interests or liberty.

(The Discourses: 394)

Monitoring is also essential because employees do not always know what the proper course of action is or what they should be doing. By knowing what they are actually doing, you are able to give them better direction and apply the proper motivation.

[T]he people often, deceived by an illusive good, desire their own ruin, and, unless they are made sensible of the evil of the one and the benefit of the other course by someone in whom they have confidence, they will expose the republic to infinite peril and damage.

(The Discourses: 204)

KNOW YOUR EMPLOYEES' NEEDS

When giving direction, it is important to make it clear that it comes from you, their leader, not from an outside source. A wise manager will constantly be aware of what his staff's needs are, both individually and as a group. A method of doing this is to hold group meetings with them. However, do not always rely on group meetings. You should spend time talking to each staff member on an individual basis.

It can also be helpful to have a suggestion box in which employees can make anonymous suggestions, but be aware that an anonymous suggestion is not as valuable as a suggestion made in person by a staff member. By knowing who is making suggestions, you are better able to judge the validity of the suggestions.

By meeting the needs of your staff, you become more secure from both internal and external threats to your power. If you study these needs, you will find that most are reasonable and easy to satisfy.

A prince, then, who wishes the good will of a people that is hostile to him [especially those who have been ruled by tyrants] should first of all ascertain what the people really desire, and he will always find that they want two things: one, to revenge themselves on those who have been the cause of their enslavement, and the other, to recover their liberty.

(The Discourses: 139)

REWARD GOOD WORK

Your staff should be rewarded for its good work and good actions, and you should always confer on its members the benefits they deserve. Indeed, this recognition will arouse in them a sense of loyalty, and they will be more helpful to you in times of conflict. Do not err by deferring these benefits in the hopes of using them as a motivation tool in times of trouble.

[L]et no one . . . defer securing the good will of the people until the moment of danger; for they will never succeed in it. . . . For the masses will think that they do not owe the benefits you have bestowed upon them to you, but to your adversaries; and fearing that, when the danger is past, you will again take from them what under the pressure of danger you conceded to them, they will feel under no obligations to you.

(The Discourses: 165–66)

A wise manager knows how to make a virtue of necessity.

The ancient commanders of armies, who well knew the powerful influence of necessity, and how it inspired the soldiers with the most desperate courage, neglected nothing to subject their men to such a pressure, [while] on the other hand, they employed every device that ingenuity could suggest to relieve the enemy's troops from the necessity of fighting.

(The Discourses: 361)

PUNISH POOR PERFORMANCE

To ensure that your staff remains motivated, and that an attitude of fairness, justice, and discipline are maintained, just as you should not withhold benefits, you should not withhold punishment.

When you punish, you must do so out of concern both for staff members' individual growth and for the growth of the organization. Just as a parent punishes out of love, a wise manager punishes out of concern.

When punishing, it is important that the punishment be equal to the offense. Most employees have a keen sense of fairness, and their unfavorable reaction to an unfair punishment will harm you, not help you. However, when there are extraordinary offenses, there is the need for extraordinary punishments.

[I]n a great republic there are constantly evils occurring requiring remedies which must be efficacious in proportion to the importance of the occasion.

(The Discourses: 429)

A managerial problem arises when selecting group punishment for the acts of the one or the many. Since much work is performed by teams, it is often difficult to pinpoint responsibility for errors. When you can, it is always more effective to punish individuals for individual actions, and not punish the group as a whole for the actions of an individual. However, at times it is not clear who should be punished for the actions of a group. Therefore, a fair method of distributing group punishment must be sought.

For when any crime is committed by a multitude, where the individual authors cannot be ascertained, it is impossible to punish them all, there being so many. To chastise a part, leaving the others unpunished, would be unjust to the first, [while] the others would feel encouraged to commit fresh crimes. But where all have merited death, and only every tenth man is punished by lot, these will have occasion to complain only of fate; [while] those who escape will be careful not to commit other crimes, for fear that the next time the lot might fall to them.

(The Discourses: 430)

MERITS DO NOT CANCEL DEMERITS

You should never be led into the trap of accepting sloppy work from employees because at some time in the past they performed good work. This is true in accepting the work of both low-level and high-level employees. If you do this, it defeats the whole purpose of fairness and justice, and the only result will be that the individual will begin to believe that he can get away with poor performance.

[N]o well ordered republic should ever cancel the crimes of its citizens by their merits; but having established rewards for good action and penalties for evil ones, and having rewarded a citizen for good conduct who afterwards commits a wrong, he should be chastised for that without regard to his previous merits. And a state that properly observes this principle will long enjoy its liberty; but if otherwise, it will speedily come to ruin.

(The Discourses: 153)

If in fact you permit poor work to be accepted from anyone, you are inviting disaster to yourself and to your organization, and eventually you will lose total control of your staff's standards of performance.

For if a citizen who has rendered some eminent service to the state should add to the reputation and influence which he has thereby acquired the confident audacity of being able to commit any wrong without fear of punishment, he will in a little while become so insolent and overbearing as to put an end to all power of the law.

(The Discourses: 153)

JUSTICE FOR ALL

A system of rewards and punishments requires also a system of justice. Employees and staff demand justice, and at times, when they have been wronged, they demand vengeance. The amount and type of vengeance allowed should be what you have decided is just and not merely a reaction to what they want. If you let them seek their own vengeance, or let them select the acts of vengeance, you will likewise lose control.

[F]inding himself placed between the insolence of the nobles on the one hand, whom he could in no way content or control, and the rage of the popular faction on the other hand, who could not support the loss of their liberty, [he] resolved suddenly to rid himself of the [persistent demands] of the nobles, and to secure to himself the good will and support of the people. Availing of a favorable opportunity, he had all the nobles massacred, to the extreme satisfaction of the people; and in this way he satisfied one of the wishes of the people, namely, the desire of revenge.

(The Discourses: 139)

Remember, employees are the key to your success, and they are the protectors of your power. It is a wise manager who nurtures his staff and is concerned about its members' personal development.

13
Religion

[T]hey are acquired either by merit or by good fortune, but are maintained without either; being upheld by the venerable ordinances of religion, which are all of such a nature and efficacy that they secure the authority of their princes in whatever way they may act or live.

(The Prince: 78)

One of the most difficult organizations to criticize or control is the religious organization. This lies in the fact that the truly detestable ones hide behind the banner of truth and righteousness. Observation of these organizations and their leaders causes even the most religious persons to question their legitimacy. But at the same time there are many religious organizations and leaders that are just in their affairs and are worthy of respect.

Of all men who have been eulogized, those deserve it most who have been the authors and founders of religions.

(The Discourses: 122)

Since religious organizations are held in such high respect, those who dare criticize or oppose their institutions are in turn criticized by others.

[T]hose are doomed to infamy and universal execration who have destroyed religions, who have overturned republics and kingdoms, who are enemies of virtue, of letters, and of every art that is useful and honorable to mankind. Such are the impious and violent, the ignorant, the idle, the vile and degraded.

(*The Discourses*: 122–23)

KNOW THE DIFFERENCE

The difficulty, of course, lies in differentiating between religious organizations and true religion.

[I]f the Christian religion had from the beginning been maintained according to the principles of its founder, the Christian states and republics would have been much more united and happy than what they are.

(*The Discourses*: 130)

It is obvious that many religious leaders through their conduct and actions, in both the contemporary age and in antiquity, have given religious institutions an evil name. Some religious leaders throughout the centuries have been conspicuous not by their righteousness, but by their misdeeds and licentious behavior. And there have been religious leaders of the twentieth century whose misdeeds are competitive with those of some infamous religious leaders of the middle ages.

Nor can there be a greater proof of its decadence than to witness the fact that the nearer people are to the Church . . . the less religious are they.

(*The Discourses*: 130)

Another difficulty is not in the religious institutions themselves, nor their goals, but rather in the leaders that people put their trust in. However, it is not proper to judge all religious leaders or organizations by the actions of a few.

[W]ith regard to religions we . . . see that revivals are equally necessary, and the best proof of this is furnished by our own, which would have been entirely lost had it not been brought back to its pristine principles and purity. . . . The new orders which they established were so severe and powerful that they became the means of saving religion from being destroyed by the licentiousness of the prelates and heads of the Church.

(*The Discourses*: 322)

THE MANAGER AND RELIGION

The nature and purpose of religion is so universal that it is important for a leader of an organization to follow and uphold the basic principles of a religion, which will sustain him either directly or indirectly.

It is therefore the duty of princes and heads of republics to uphold the foundations of the religion of their countries, for then it is easy to keep their people
religious, and consequently well conducted and united. And therefore everything
that tends to favor religion (even though it were believed to be false) should be
received and availed of to strengthen it; and this should be done the more, the
wiser the rulers are, and the better they understand the natural course of things.

(*The Discourses*: 129)

Thus, it is well to seem merciful, faithful, humane, religious, and upright, and
also to be so; but the mind should remain so balanced that were it needful not
to be so, you should be able and know how to change to the contrary.

(*The Prince*: 128)

Therefore, an important characteristic that all managers should acquire
is at least a semblance of religious virtue and social consciousness. And
while these statements are true for almost all managers, they are especially
true for those leaders who organize and develop political organizations.
Political leaders who are without religious roots are subject to disrepute
among those whom they would lead.

A wise manager considers the nature and purpose of religion and the
way it fits into his organizational life.

14

Fortresses

[A] new Prince has [never] disarmed his subjects. On the contrary, when he has found them unarmed he has always armed them. For the arms thus provided become yours, those whom you suspected grow faithful, while those who were faithful at the first, continue so, and . . . your subjects become your partisans.

(The Prince: 154)

A manager can be put in personal danger in many ways, and you must always take necessary precautions to protect yourself. Danger can come from a variety of sources—embittered employees, relatives of employees, opponents, dissatisfied customers, or unknown persons. Danger can be both physical and psychological, and it can on rare occasions result in serious and even fatal injury. A manager should also assure that other members in the organization are protected from danger. This is done by taking reasonable and necessary security measures for both yourself and your employees.

PROTECTING YOURSELF

The higher your position in an organization the more physical security you need. However, you should not have so much protection and physical separation that you become isolated in an ivory tower away from your employees.

[T]he object of fortresses, [is to serve] as a means of defense against a foreign enemy as well as against one's own subjects. In the first case . . . they are unnecessary, and in the second decidedly injurious.

(*The Discourses*: 293)

As an individual rises in the management ranks, there is a tendency to restrict access to himself from both staff and customers.

[B]ut being a very sagacious man, and knowing that it was the good will of the people, and not fortresses, that maintain princes in their states, he had the citadel destroyed. And thus, instead of founding his state upon the strength of the fortress, but upon his valor and prudence, he [held his position].

(*The Discourses*: 296)

DO NOT FEAR YOUR EMPLOYEES

The more you fear your employees the more you withdraw from them, and the more you withdraw from them the more they begin to distrust you. And that distrust can turn into hatred.

[W]henever either princes or republics are afraid lest their subjects should revolt, it results mainly from the hatred of the subjects on account of the bad treatment experienced from those who govern them; and this comes either from the belief that they can best be controlled by force, or from lack of sound judgment in governing them. And one of the things that induce the belief that they can be controlled by force is the possession of fortresses with which to menace them.

(*The Discourses*: 293)

It is also a wise course of action to make yourself available to customers of the organization—whether they be internal or external. This ensures that you keep current with the way others feel your organization is doing. You also need be aware of customers' attitudes so you can take the actions that are necessary to correct matters should there be problems. No manager has ever been able to isolate himself within his organization completely without being destroyed either by a conspiracy from within or from attack by opponents outside the organization.

If you build fortresses they may serve in time of peace to encourage you to oppress your subjects; but in time of war they are most useless, because they will be assailed by the enemy as well as by your subjects, and cannot possibly resist both.

(*The Discourses*: 294)

FIND SUPPORTERS

One of the best methods of providing for your security is to develop employees who are loyal to you. Indeed, there is nothing that provides better security than loyal employees. When first taking control of an organization, do not be too quick to judge who is loyal and who is not, who will be helpful and who will not.

[M]anagers, and new [Managers] especially, have found greater [loyalty] and helpfulness in those whom, at the beginning of their reign, they held in suspicion, than in those who at the outset have had their confidence . . . [The manager] who acquires a new [organization] through the favor of its inhabitants, [should] weigh well what were the causes which led those who favored him to do so; and if it be seen that they have acted not from any natural affection for him, but merely out of discontent with the former government, . . . he will find the utmost difficulty in keeping them his friends, since it will be impossible for him to . . . [make them happy].

(The Prince: 158)

[T]he Prince who is more afraid of his subjects than of strangers should build fortresses, while he who is more afraid of strangers than of his subjects, should leave them alone.

(The Prince: 160)

THE PROTECTION OF LOVE

While many managers are afraid to say they love their employees or that they desire love from them, either because they do not love them or because they are embarrassed by the word, a manager will find that when loyalty is turned into love he has acquired the greatest protection of all. He has done more than just avoid hatred.

[T]he best fortress you can have, is in not being hated by your subjects. If they hate you, no fortress will save you; for when once the people take up arms, foreigners are never wanting to assist them.

(The Prince: 161)

I shall applaud him who builds fortresses, and him who does not; but I shall blame him who, trusting in them, reckons it a light thing to be held in hatred by his people.

(The Prince: 162)

A wise manager recognizes both the necessity and the limit of seclusion and through thought and practice is able to maintain the proper balance between them.

15
Types of Leaders

[I]t is a certain rule, that he who gives severe orders must see them executed with severity, otherwise he will find himself deceived. . . . he who wishes to be obeyed must know how to command; and those give proof of knowing this who properly estimate their own strength with reference to that of those who have to obey, and who command only when he finds them to bear a proper proportion to each other, and who abstains from commanding when that proportion is [lacking].

(*The Discourses*: 382)

As I have said before, management is getting things done through people. Douglas McGregor classified managers into two basic types: Theory X and Theory Y.

THEORY X

A manager is classified as a Theory X manager if he believes that the average worker is lazy and must be forced to work and controlled with punishment. Theory X managers also believe that the average worker avoids responsibility, prefers to be directed, lacks ambition, and values security most of all. Theory X managers include those who impose their decisions on subordinates and motivate employees by threat alone.

[S]o that surrounded by these he may be able to maintain his power, and that by his support they may satisfy their ambition, and the others may be constrained to submit to that yoke to which force alone has been able to subject them.

(The Discourses: 211)

While theoreticians find comfort voicing their displeasure about Theory X managers, a wise manager knows from observation that there are many people in organizations who fit this definition. And what the studies of the theoreticians fail to account for, and what they fail to tell you, is how to motivate workers who do fit this category. Force may not be your first choice, but it may become the only choice.

If a job is not getting done properly, force may become necessary. And when it becomes necessary, you must use force power both effectively and efficiently. If the task is important, then apply it with vigor. After the problem is solved, you can make an analysis of why it was necessary to use force power, as opposed to one of the other types of power, and seek other ways of motivating the workers.

[But to do the extraordinary] requires a man of rare genius and power, and therefore out of the many that have attempted it but few have succeeded; for the greatness of the enterprise frightens men so that they fail even in the very beginning.

(The Discourses: 211)

THEORY Y

The opposite of a Theory X manager is called Theory Y. If you are a Theory Y manager you believe that individuals think of work as natural, like play or rest. You believe that people will exercise self-direction and are self-controlled in seeking to accomplish the objectives to which they are committed. You also believe that given the right conditions, the average worker can learn to accept and to seek responsibility. Theory Y managers believe that the capacity for creativity in solving organizational problems resides in many workers.

[I]t is always well in a state that every one may propose what he deems for the public good; and it [is] equally well that everyone should be allowed to express his opinion in relation to it, so that the people, having heard both sides, may decide in favor of the best.

(The Discourses: 144–45)

While some employees may exhibit some of these characteristics, however, they are neither the average employee, nor the only employee the manager has to motivate. And some of those who do have these qualities are as interested in being the manager as they are interested in doing a good job. This may or may not be in your best interest. If you manage such employees, they are the ones that you should above all nurture loyalty in.

OTHER CLASSIFICATIONS OF MANAGERS

It is unfortunate when making distinctions between types of managers that convenient tags are not posted over their office doors so that one can be distinguished from the other. While a manager may practice Theory X or Theory Y behavior, the world of management is far from being clearly divided into two discrete types of managers. For there is no such thing as the perfect worker or the perfect manager.

Managers have been classified and reclassified over the years, with so many different names that it becomes unclear which name means what. At times the name used interferes with understanding what it is the manager does.

Some managers are condescending; some are trusting; some are autocratic; some are participative. Some care little about either getting the job done or about the people who do the job. Nor do they care about the needs of the organization. Often this type of manager is counting the days until his retirement.

Some managers care a lot about doing the job, but care little about those who do it. They are proud of the accomplishments of their staffs, but they fail to communicate effectively with them.

Some managers care little about getting the job done, but they care a lot about the people who do the job. This type of manager likes to be liked, and spends more time in staff development activities than in motivating his staff to do an effective job.

Another type of manager tries to have the best of both worlds. He tries to walk the middle of the road. He shows a moderate amount of concern about both getting the job done and the people who do the job.

But men generally decide upon a middle course, which is most hazardous; for they know neither how to be entirely good or entirely bad.

(The Discourses: 156)

Some managers have both a high concern for getting the job done and a high concern for the people who do the job. They try to do the impossible by being equally concerned about organizational and staff matters and often fail in both.

Another type of manager has a low concern for both doing the job and the people who do the job, but loves rules. Such managers are interested in policies and procedures to control organizational situations and spend their work day counting things—being more concerned about the how instead of the why. This type of manager is considered a bureaucrat and can be found in both the private and public sectors.

There are other managers who have a high concern for getting the job done but never get involved in the work themselves.

The last type of manager appears to have a high concern for the way the job is done and a high concern for the people who do the job, but this concern is often shallow, and he communicates in riddles. This everything-is-wonderful manager is often counterproductive and very likely to misconstrue reality, thereby failing to know when problems are to be solved.

On your journey to success it is necessary to become familiar with the characteristics and motivations of all the various types of managers, because some of them will be opponents of your empire, as they try to increase their empires. And by understanding them you will be better prepared to do battle with them.

THE THEORY M MANAGER

While some of these managers have good qualities and some have bad, none of them are ideal, nor are they what you should strive for if you desire power and success. The ideal manager is called the Theory M manager. This manager recognizes that it is necessary to employ a variety of tactics for varying management situations. He is confident in his leadership abilities and understands both the scientific and artistic sides of management. He recognizes that power consists of many separate components and can select the right type of power, or combination of power, for the proper situation.

[H]e who carries too far the desire to make himself beloved will soon become contemned, if he deviates in the slightest degree from the true path; and the other, who aims at making himself feared, will make himself hated, if he goes in the least degree too far; and our nature does not permit us always to keep the just middle course. Either extreme, therefore, must be compensated for by some extraordinary merits.

(*The Discourses*: 379)

The Theory M manager is concerned about the organization and has a high degree of concern for his staff members, but does not let the concern for one aspect distract him from the other. He develops leadership patterns that enable him to be a highly effective and efficient manager.

He uses the motivation that is necessary to get a job done and instills in employees the confidence that they can do the job. In making decisions he assesses and analyzes the present situation, circumstances and other environmental factors, and after the analysis he makes an immediate decision, not procrastinating. He recognizes that environmental factors change and constantly need assessing.

[T]here are two ways of contending, one in accordance with the laws, the other by force; the first of which is proper to men, the second to beasts. But since the first method is often ineffectual, it becomes necessary to resort to the second. A Prince should, therefore, understand how to use well both the man and the beast . . . and that the one without the other has no stability.

(*The Prince*: 125–26)

On this . . . depend the shifts of Fortune. For if to one who conducts himself with caution and patience, time and circumstance are [favorable], so that his method of acting is good, he goes on prospering; but if these change he is ruined, because he does not change his method of acting.

(*The Prince*: 186–87)

It is necessary also that they should esteem their general, and have confidence in his ability; and this will not fail to be the case when they see him orderly, watchful, and courageous, and that he maintains the dignity of his rank by a proper reputation. All this he will do by punishing faults, by not fatiguing his troops unnecessarily, by strictly fulfilling his promises, by showing them that victory is easy, and by concealing or making light of the dangers which he discerns from afar. These maxims well observed are the best means of inspiring the troops with that confidence which is the surest pledge of victory.

(*The Discourses*: 404)

ADAPTING TO CHANGE

The Theory M manager recognizes that different workers have different motivations and that these attitudes change with time. He knows every worker is an individual and that each thinks differently, and that work is not as much fun for some as it is for others. He knows that varying facts call for varying actions. He realizes that dynamic technology affects both workers and managers, and that the introduction of new technology in the organization calls for a reappraisal of his management style. And the Theory M manager acknowledges that, as I have discussed in Chapter 4, there are five components of power—Alpha, Beta, Gamma, Theta, and Omega—and that to be effective he must use each in the precise amount at the appropriate time.

[T]o give vigorous orders requires a vigorous mind; and he who has that strength of mind, and commands, cannot enforce the execution of his order by gentle means. And he who lacks such vigor of mind must be careful not to order anything extraordinary; but in ordinary matters he may act with his natural gentleness, for ordinary punishments are not imputed to the prince, but to the laws and the necessity of preserving order.

(*The Discourses*: 382)

The Theory M manager is not Machiavellian in the popular sense of the word, the evil sense, and he is certainly never cruel in his actions. Indeed, he is caring and concerned about his employees and uses those Machiavellian principles that are necessary to accomplish the task of the organization and assist him in reaching his goals. He does as Machiavelli would have done, and adds to the ancient principles of leadership and victory the lessons of present. He has translated the original Machiavellian ideas into ideas that make sense in today's business and organizational world.

Even the Theory M manager is not perfect, because it is never easy to be a great manager, but if you strive to maintain the above qualities you will have your share of management successes.

Located in the appendix is a Machiavellian orientation inventory designed to measure your M factor, or the degree to which you have Machiavellian tendencies.

16
Management Devices

[T]here is no quality so self-destructive as liberality; for while you practice it you lose the means whereby it can be practiced, and become
poor and despised, or else, to avoid poverty, you become rapacious
and hated. For liberality leads to one or other of these two results,
against which, beyond all others, a Prince should guard. Wherefore
it is wiser to put up with the name of being [stingy], which breeds
[disgrace], but without hate, than be obliged, from the desire to be
reckoned liberal, to incur the reproach of [greed], which breeds both
hate and [disgrace].

(*The Prince*: 117)

Not only are there various types of managers, but there are various styles
of managing. These styles can be used by any of the different types of
managers at any time. And just as in selecting the type of manager you
wish to be, you can select the methods you wish to use. The difference
between management type and management style is analogous to the
difference between an individual's personality and his actions. While
sometimes they seem the same, often they contradict each other. It is often
easier to see what a person does—his style—than it is to perceive who
he is—his type. Your management type is fundamental to who you are,
while your management style is represented by your actions.

Just as your style of management should change with the situation, so
should your method of managing. No one method, by itself, is better than
any other, and each has its place within a given environment. While most

managers tend to utilize only one style of management, the Theory M manager will use attributes of each style, depending on the situation, since he is more concerned about meeting the management challenge, which requires solving problems and making decisions in situations of change and uncertainty. And the more creative he becomes, the better able he is to use several styles concurrently.

MANAGEMENT BY APPEARANCE

The first method is called management by appearance.

He who desires or attempts to reform the government of a state, and wishes to have it accepted and capable of maintaining itself to the satisfaction of everybody, must at least retain the semblance of the old forms; so that it may seem to the people that there has been no change in the institutions, even though in fact they are entirely different from the old ones. For the great majority of mankind are satisfied with appearances, as though they were realities, and are often even more influenced by the things that seem than by those that are.

(*The Discourses*: 154)

It is a maxim of management that people will resist change even when it is for the better. So since employees will resist management changes—by using management by appearance—you can invoke change without calling it change. One way of doing this is to change the functions of a division without changing its name. You might even keep a person on staff for a period of time after instituting staffing changes, yet give them no real job to do. This helps maintain the illusion that nothing has changed. In this manner people remain comfortable because things appear to be the same. The adage that what you see is not necessarily what you get becomes the operating method.

It is not essential, then, that a Prince should have all the good qualities . . . [telling the truth, acting uprightly and not craftily], but it is essential that he should seem to have them . . . [I]f he has and invariably practices them all, they are hurtful, whereas the appearance of having them is useful.

(*The Prince*: 128)

It should be noted that management by appearance, while not impossible, is more difficult when you are dealing with higher-level staff, whose higher-level abilities will allow them to penetrate many smoke screens.

Artifices . . . are quickly [seen] by the wise, but the people are generally deceived by them. Blinded by their eager desire for present peace, they do not see the snares that are concealed under . . . [generous] promises.

(*The Discourses*: 362)

If you are challenged, once you have made changes by this method, you must never admit that things are different. Insist that those who challenge this are imagining things and that what you say is what they see.

MANAGEMENT BY POPULARITY

Management by being popular, while a weak method, is sometimes important in reaching short-term objectives. While this is primarily a management method, being popular is also used by subordinates as a method of being managed.

[I]ts attainment depends not wholly on merit, nor wholly on good fortune, but rather on a fortunate astuteness [cleverness and opportunity] . . . [It is gained] either through the favor of the people or of the nobles.

(*The Prince*: 65)

When using this method your objective is to keep people happy by trying to meet all their happiness needs. You do what makes people feel good, and not necessarily what is good for them or good for the organization. Using this method may lessen their complaining about situations or problems, and it will relieve some of the immediate pressure on you, thereby serving your short-term objectives.

[T]he Roman people no longer [bestowed] the consulate according to the merits of the candidates, but according to favor; giving that dignity to those who best knew how to entertain the people, and not to those who best know how to conquer their enemies.

(*The Discourses*: 144)

MANAGEMENT BY AVOIDANCE

The problems you avoid—management by avoidance—usually do not get solved, and they compound the structural problems within the organization. Neither management by popularity nor management by avoidance should be used as a long-term strategy, because eventually they will cause you to lose control of your organization. You cannot avoid problems forever, nor can you constantly make employees happy. Some days it rains.

[Since] it is difficult to know . . . evils at their first origin, owing to an illusion which all new things are apt to produce, the wiser course is to temporize with such evils when they are recognized, instead of violently attacking them; for by temporizing with them they will either die out of themselves, or at least their worst results will be long deferred.

(*The Discourses*: 168)

[A] general who wishes to keep the field cannot avoid a battle when the enemy is determined upon fighting.

(The Discourses: 356)

[Y]ou ought never to [allow] your designs to be crossed in order to avoid war, since war is not so to be avoided, but is only deferred to your disadvantage.

(The Prince: 19)

MANAGEMENT BY COMMITTEE

Management by committee is used in situations where you desire to delay decisions, without the reason for the delay being your responsibility. Depending on the formation of the committee and the nature of the decisions, it is possible that the use of this method will give you tremendous lengths of time in which to drag out the decision-making process.

The Ten bore themselves very civilly and modestly, having but ten lictors to walk before him whom they had elected to preside over them; and although they had absolute authority, yet when they had occasion to punish a Roman citizen for homicide, they cited him before the people and made them judge him. These . . . wrote their laws upon ten tablets, and before finally confirming them exposed them in public, in order that they might be read and discussed by everybody, and that they might learn whether the laws were in any way defective, so that they might be amended before their final confirmation. Hereupon Appius caused a rumor to be circulated throughout Rome, that, if two more tablets were added to the ten, the laws would be still more perfect, so that this opinion, generally accredited, afforded the people the opportunity to reappoint the Ten for another year, of which they readily availed.

(The Discourses: 182–83)

This method is also best used as a short-term strategy. While the committee is struggling with the issue, you can be making plans to resolve the situation or problem. However, extended use of the method can result in loss of your power and control. But if you are the appointing source and in you alone lies the power to dispose of the committee at will, then its value is greatly increased.

MANAGEMENT BY CONFLICT

Management by conflict is a method by which you design an organization consisting of subunits with conflicting goals. As the performance of one subunit increases, the performance of the other decreases. And you design the organization in such a manner that it is structurally impossible for one subunit to perform its job without the assistance of the other. It is also helpful to build into the design reporting relationships that cause the various subordinates' jobs to continually conflict with each other. You do this by purposefully making their actual responsibilities and duties unclear.

[F]or all the measures of force and violence that you employ to hold a people amount to nothing, except these two: either you must keep a good army always ready to take the field . . . or you must scatter, disorganize, and destroy the people so completely that they can in no way injure you.

(*The Discourses*: 293–94)

This method is used more often than not by managers who are unsure of their own strength within the organization. However, there are circumstances when *divide et impera*—the maxim of the Romans—can be useful. It especially becomes necessary to use this method when your superior managers have already designed the organization to operate in that manner. While this may not be your choice of an operating style, in this case you may be forced to adopt it in an attempt to counteract the conflict situations that have been imposed on you.

If the subordinates you involve in the structure are weak, the conflict prevents them from forming any type of conspiracy or power grab, because they will lack trust in each other and each other's ideas. If they are strong, however, there is a chance that this strategy could spawn a conspiracy by making their job so difficult that the only way they believe they can survive is to overthrow you. This difficulty can be almost totally controlled by designing the organization to be a convoluted paradox organization. This happens when you involve an odd number of subordinates in the conflict, usually three or five. This will make it difficult for the conspirators to reach a decision. If you involve more than five, it is likely that a power bloc can be created from among the various factions and that the bloc will be able to take a lead in conspiratorial actions. The best solution is to make the conflict a three-way situation. In this manner, when there is no consensus there will always be at least one person or group isolated. For this purpose you must design the structure so that even two working against the one is advantageous to no one.

However, a wise manager realizes that consistent conflict can work to his disadvantage.

[They] began with insults and attacks to abuse and offend the Romans, with such a degree of [audacity] and insolence that it caused the Romans to forget their dissensions and to become united; so that when it came to a regular battle . . . the Romans completely defeated and routed them. This shows how apt men are to deceive themselves . . . in deciding upon what course they are to take, and how frequently they lose where they had confidently hoped to win.

(*The Discourses*: 299)

MANAGEMENT BY WALKING AROUND

Management by walking around is a desirable style when used in moderation. It not only gives staff and employees an opportunity to see their leader, and thereby increase their awareness of him, but it also gives the leader an opportunity to see what activities are taking place in the organization. It assists him in finding answers to such important management questions as What is going on that you aren't being told? and What isn't going on that you thought was? And it is a good method of gathering intelligence. You can employ management by walking around in both formal and informal situations.

He ought, moreover, at suitable seasons of the year to entertain the people with festivals and shows . . . [h]e should show attention . . . [to all groups in the organization] and sometimes take part in their meetings; offering an example of courtesy and munificence, but always maintaining the dignity of his station, which must under no circumstances be compromised.

(The Prince: 170)

Caesar and Alexander and all the valiant and brave Princes were always at the head of their Armies, completely armed and on foot, and rather than lose their [organizations] they would lose their lives; so as they lived and died with a great deal of honor.

(The Art of War: 523)

The last four styles of management—management by force, management by fear, management by tyranny, and management by love—will be discussed in the next chapter.

17
Being Loved or Feared

A Prince should therefore . . . [not mind being called cruel] where it enables him to keep his subjects united and faithful. For he who quells disorder by a very few signal examples will in the end be more merciful than he who from excessive leniency suffers things to take their course and so result in rapine and bloodshed; for these hurt the entire State, whereas the severities of the Prince injure individuals only. And for a new Prince, above all others, it is impossible to escape a name for cruelty, since new States are full of dangers.

(*The Prince*: 118–19)

Of the remaining methods of managing are management by fear, management by force, management by tyranny, and management by love.

MANAGEMENT BY TYRANNY

Management by tyranny is the unscrupulous use of power within an organization, and it is usually pursued by managers who are greedy and overly confident—usually when they have nothing to be confident about. A characteristic of such managers is lack of social conscience or false social conscience. This management method is damaging not only to the manager's subunit, but also to the organization as a whole. When a manager practices management by tyranny in the extreme, it is often necessary for the organization or state to punish him. This can be done by an organization through demotion, transfer, or termination. A state may choose to censure the person through a regulatory agency or bring the person to a court of law. Punishment is sometimes also instigated by individuals—other managers or employees—who seek vengeance either singularly or by conspiracy. This vengeance is most often psychological in nature, but in the extreme it can be physical. So a wise manager will never abuse his staff.

[Tyranny was] the beginning and causes of disorders, conspiracies, and plots against the sovereigns, set on foot, not by the feeble and timid, but by those citizens who, surpassing the others in grandeur of soul, in wealth, and in courage, could not submit to the outrages and excesses of their princes.

(The Discourses: 100–101)

A form of management by tyranny is used by workers in an organization who have interaction with customers. These pseudo-managers make it difficult for customers to deal with an organization, especially when they have a complaint to lodge concerning services provided by the organization or the conduct of employees within the organization. This characteristic can be found in both government and corporate bureaucrats and in those who act like bureaucrats. And just as managers who practice management by tyranny should be rooted from the organization, likewise, employees who practice tyranny over customers should be discharged. An extremely valuable method of finding these employees is to regularly employ secret customers who make regular contact with employees, posing as real customers, and then file reports of their encounters with the management of the organization. If employees believe that any customer they serve could be reporting on their actions, they probably serve the organization and the manager better.

MANAGEMENT BY FEAR

If they are the only methods used by a manager, management by fear and management by force are related to Theory X. They are related to Theory M if they are among a variety of methods a manager uses in his arsenal of weapons. In using management by fear effectively, you must be sure that your subordinates are aware that there are not only rewards for good behavior, but also punishments for bad behavior.

However, these punishments must always be fair, because their purpose is not to punish for punishment's sake, but to instill a sense of discipline among employees and staff. Any punishment you have to use should not be meted out at random or without warning and never without cause. Policies, procedures, and other organizational rules must clearly spell out the consequences of violation, especially when the consequences are negative. If a manager uses too much force or fear, it will generally cause him great distress because of its negative nature—in effect, he is also punished through his excesses.

A wise manager, as opposed to a purely tyrannical manager, would rather not enforce punishments but knows at times it is necessary. He also knows that to be effective, punishment must be sure and swift. Delayed punishment is worse than no punishment at all. If you are delinquent in using punishment, then it is best not to use it at all.

[E]very Prince should desire to be accounted merciful and not cruel. Nevertheless, he should be careful not to abuse this quality of mercy.

(*The Prince*: 118)

The methods of managing by fear and force are hardest for new managers. When they manage in this manner they believe that employees and staff will only dislike them. They tend to operate in the management-by-being-popular mode at the beginning of their management career, believing this to be the road to success and happiness. However, to be effective a new manager must be willing to use force and punishment even more than a tenured one.

When a new manager enters an organization, he is often tested by employees to see how much latitude of action is available to him. If he is perceived as weak, the defiant will attempt to acquire some of his power. If he loses power to them because of this, eventually, the manager will also be perceived as weak by other managers in the organization, and in a short time he will also be attacked by them. And in time he will have lost all of his foundation for organizational survival.

[T]he new Prince should not be too ready of belief, nor too easily set in motion; nor should he himself be the first to raise alarms; but should so temper prudence with kindliness that too great confidence in others shall not throw him off his guard, nor groundless distrust render him insupportable.

(*The Prince*: 119)

MANAGEMENT BY FORCE

Management by force can either be used in conjunction with management by fear or by itself. As with fear, force as a management tool must also be used with caution. However, this does not mean that force should be used only as a last resort, but rather only when the situation clearly calls for it.

And if constrained to put anyone to death, he should do so only when there is manifest cause or reasonable justification. But, above all, he must abstain from . . . [taking the benefits] of others. For men will sooner forget the death of their father than the loss of their patrimony.

(The Prince: 121)

The force a manager uses is psychological as opposed to physical. It is the optimum use of your will over the will of your employees, and it is as much a presence of spirit as it is any set of tangible actions. It is the acceptance by others that in any confrontation you will prevail, and that therefore it is to their advantage to avoid confrontations with you. Your opponents then interpret your total power to be greater than theirs and therefore they, too, avoid confrontation.

[A]nd fear restrained all the others from speaking against such laws; and thus the people were by force and fraud made to resolve upon their own ruin.

(The Discourses: 145)

USE ONLY MODERATE FEAR AND FORCE

I cannot overemphasize the importance of using both fear and force only in moderation, and only when the situation demands it. I also must reiterate that they should always be just and fair. If a situation arises in which you are having to use an excess of management by fear or force with an employee or a group of employees, it is a sign of weakness in your style of management or in the organizational structure.

But he who has to command subjects . . . should employ severity rather than gentleness, lest these subjects should become insolent, and trample his authority under foot, because of too great indulgence. This severity, however, should be employed with moderation, so as to avoid making yourself odious, for no prince is ever benefited by making himself hated.

(The Discourses: 376)

If your excess of management by force is from weakness of style, it behooves you to take immediate corrective action and change that style. If the organizational structure is at fault, the weakness can only be corrected by making policy changes that effect change in organizational procedures or design, or by readjusting the duties and relationships of staff members.

However, at times problems can only be corrected by either the termination of yourself or the employee(s) in conflict. If that is the solution, then the obvious goal should be the termination of the employees in conflict—not you. If a constant atmosphere of force exists between a manager and an employee, this will in turn disaffect other employees and damage the organization as a whole. Therefore, when termination is called for, do not hesitate; if you do, you lose.

MANAGEMENT BY LOVE

Both management by force and management by fear are damaging to the manager when used in excess. Your goal should be to create an organization in which love is present, both that which is given by you and that which is received from employees, and a minimum of coercive power is used.

[B]eing loved depends upon his subjects, while his being feared depends upon himself, a wise Prince should build on what is his own, and not what rests with others. . . . [H]e must do his best to escape hatred.

(The Prince: 124)

But while your desire is for love, you should never sacrifice the needs of the organization for the sake of receiving it.

[W]e should wish to be both [feared and loved]; but since love and fear can hardly exist together, if we must choose between them, it is far safer to be feared than loved.

(The Prince: 120)

If you create an organization in which the many styles of management are used in the appropriate situations, an organization in which fairness and justice are present, you will have created an environment in which you and your staff are in harmony. In this situation the proper amount of management and staff love will be present. Always remember that your staff and employees are the key to an effective organization.

[T]he best fortress you can have, is in not being hated by your subjects.

(The Prince: 161)

For although [money, the current situation, and the good disposition of your staff] will increase [your] strength, yet they will not give it to [you], and of themselves are nothing, and will be of no use without a devoted army. Neither abundance nor natural strength of the country will suffice, nor will the loyalty and good will of his subjects endure, for these cannot remain faithful to a prince who is incapable of defending them.

(The Discourses: 251)

18

Gaining a Reputation

Nor let it be supposed that any [organization] can choose for itself a perfectly safe line of conduct. On the contrary, it must reckon on every course it may take [as] being doubtful; for it happens in all human affairs that we never seek to escape one mischief without falling into another. Prudence therefore consists in knowing how to distinguish degrees of disadvantage, and in accepting a less evil as a good.

(The Prince: 169)

Success is reaching your goals while at the same time maintaining your values and relationships with those who are important to you—your significant others. If you reach your goals by compromising your values, then victory becomes hollow. If you reach your goals at the cost of losing relationships with those you care about, the result is defeat clothed in the garment of victory.

SHARE YOUR SUCCESS

Your successes belong to you and yours, but it is unseemly for you to gloat over them. Yet, success kept in a closet is of no value. If you are going to climb the management ladder of prosperity, others in the organization must know that you are wise and capable. Achieving victories increases the confidence your subordinates have in you; they increase the respect your superiors have for you, and they cause your opponents to become fearful of you. Therefore, you must not hide them.

We often see that humility not only is of no service, but is actually hurtful, especially when employed towards insolent men, who from jealousy or some other motive have conceived a hatred against you.

(*The Discourses*: 260–61)

For win a Battle, and you cancel all your former miscarriages; lose one, and all that [you] ever . . . did well before evaporates, and comes to nothing.

(*The Art of War*: 442)

KNOW YOUR LIMITS

You should not be afraid to tackle any project or take on any assignment that will give you the opportunity to show your talents. Of course if your talents are limited, or if your talents do not match a project, do not take it. You do not earn an *E* for effort when you are a manager. Nor does trying hard help you. Winning and losing are the performance standards, and just as a victory will assist you, defeat will hurt you.

For when defeat comes, instead of the successes which the people expected, they charge it neither upon the ill fortune or incompetence of their leaders, but upon their wickedness and ignorance; and generally either kill, imprison, or exile them.

(*The Discourses*: 207)

But above all, [a manager] should strive by all his actions to inspire a sense of his greatness and goodness.

(*The Prince*: 165)

DECLARE YOURSELF A FRIEND OR AN ENEMY

One of the clearest actions you can take in order to gain a reputation with others is to show associates whether you are a true friend or a true enemy. If you fail to declare yourself a friend, and then act in that manner, they will deem you unworthy of friendship or be unsure of you. Likewise, you should be cautious of people who say they are your friend but don't come to your assistance when you are in trouble.

A [manager] is likewise esteemed who is a staunch friend and a thorough foe, that is to say, who without reserve openly declares for one against another, this being always a more advantageous course than to stand neutral. For supposing two of your powerful neighbors come to blows, it must either be that you have, or have not, reason to fear the one who comes off victorious. In either case it will always be well for you to declare yourself, and join in frankly with one side or other. For should you fail to do so you are certain, in the former of the cases put, to become the prey of the victor to the satisfaction and delight of the vanquished, and no reason or excuse you may plead will avail to shield or shelter you; for the victor loves not doubtful friends, and such as will not help him at a pinch; and the vanquished will have nothing to say to you, since you would not share his fortunes sword in hand.

(*The Prince*: 165–66)

To remain neutral, while seemingly a safe course, is in fact the path that managers follow on their way to folly.

And it will always happen that he who is not your friend will invite you to neutrality, while he who is your friend will call on you to declare yourself openly in arms.

(*The Prince*: 167)

Irresolute Princes, to escape immediate danger, commonly follow the neutral path, in most instances to their destruction. . . . [w]hen you pronounce valiantly in favor of one side or other, if he to whom you give your adherence conquers, although he be powerful and you are at his mercy, still he is under obligation to you, and has become your friend; and none are so lost to shame as to destroy with manifest ingratitude him who has helped them.

(*The Prince*: 167)

BE FAIR

To insure that your reputation remains sterling, it is important to be just in all your actions and decisions. And it is necessary that you be just not only to your friends but to your opponents. A manager is just because it is necessary; a leader is just because it is right.

[V]ictories are never so complete that the victor can disregard all considerations whatsoever, more especially [the need to be just].

(*The Prince*: 167)

A wise manager will always favor those who perform well on job assignments, and will reward them for their actions.

[A manager] should show himself a [lover] of merit, and should honor those who excel in any art.

(*The Prince*: 169)

If a manager wishes to be successful he is self-confident and assured, and can perform a wide variety of tasks in a consistent manner. Mixed with his self-confidence is an appropriate amount of humility, and he unquestionably respects the virtues of true friendship.

19
Cruelty

And knowing that past severities had generated ill-feeling against himself, in order to purge the minds of the people and gain their entire goodwill, he sought to show them that any cruelty which had been done had not originated with him, but in the harsh disposition of his minister. Availing himself of the pretext this afforded, he one morning caused [him] to be beheaded and exposed in the market place of Cesna with a block and bloody axe by his side—a savage spectacle which at once astounded and satisfied the populace.

(*The Prince*: 47)

In building on the foundations of an empire, it is necessary to recruit and retain a loyal staff, and after you have acquired them it is incumbent upon you to become familiar with who they are and the jobs they perform. This is important in order to be assured that they have the skills to do the tasks they are responsible for performing.

You can accomplish this by first reviewing their resumes to become familiar with the experiences they have had. Next you should have them prepare answers to a series of questions you have developed in order to learn more about their goals and motivations. After reviewing their responses, you should then have a personal interview with each person in order to become acquainted with them and to learn something of their nature and motivations. This information will benefit you as you set your goals and those of your staff—the organizational goals, because by knowing their strengths and weaknesses you will be better able to assess what they are truly capable of performing.

DEMAND THE BEST FROM YOUR STAFF

Often in maintaining or building an empire you will have staff members who, by either being incapable or unmotivated, are not able to perform up to your expectations. It is necessary that your expectations of each staff person be high, and you should be disappointed when a person fails to achieve the goals you have established for him.

I will never fight against the enemy "without your orders, not even if I were perfectly certain of victory [quoting Manlius Torquatus]." When a man of this character comes to command, he desires to have all men like himself; his vigorous character is reproduced in his orders; and these once given, he will require their strict observance.

(*The Discourses*: 381–82)

Unless your staff is as highly motivated as you are, you will have a more difficult time achieving your objectives.

USING FIRE-FIGHTERS

At times your staff will become lazy and unmotivated, regardless of what you do. Or you may not have a talent for correcting deviant organizational behavior. One method of instilling a sense of discipline and a renewed spirit is to obtain the services of an outside person to join your organization and assist in establishing a new order. This person, often called a firefighter or hatchetperson, establishes new policies, changes the order of things, and renders a new working environment; when appropriate, this outsider assists in eliminating undesirable workers.

[T]here were many who knew better how to refrain from doing wrong themselves than how to correct the wrongdoing of others.

(*The Prince*: 123)

Princes should . . . [assign to others] those matters which entail responsibility, and reserve to themselves those that relate to grace and favor. . . . [A] Prince should esteem the great, but must not make himself odious to the people.

(*The Prince*: 137–38)

By assigning unpleasant tasks to others you are better able to keep in the good graces of your staff. And just as you might blame many of the activities that people find difficult or that they disagree with on your predecessor, when the time is right you can blame any atrocities that have been committed on this person. By disposing of the firefighter at the opportune time, you will please your staff and also give an example of what can happen if they do not reach a higher standard of performance.

[T]he temper of the multitude is fickle, and that while it is easy to persuade them of a thing, it is hard to fix them in that persuasion . . . [m]atters should be so ordered that when men no longer believe of their own accord, they may be compelled to believe by force.

(*The Prince*: 36)

USE REASONABLE FORCE

For those employees still resistant to your designs, you may need to employ further force. However, just as in acquiring your empire it is important not to use excessive force, but only that force which is reasonable to the situation at hand. Draconian measures or harsh inducements should be your last choice in managing, and should be avoided wherever possible. Draconian measures are usually a sign of a manager who has little real power. However, this does not imply that you should avoid tough or strict management actions when appropriate.

Resistance you encounter in your job as a manager is usually a product of your staff being disunited, and when this is the case, it is necessary to reunite them in such a manner that you gain their confidence.

The way to do this is to try and win the confidence of the citizens that are divided [among] themselves, and to manage to become the arbiter between them, unless they should have come to arms; but having come to arms, then sparingly to favor the weaker party, so as to keep up the war and make them exhaust themselves, and not to give them occasion for the apprehension, by a display of your forces, that you intend to subject them and make yourself their prince. And if this course be well carried out, it will generally end in your obtaining the object you aim at.

(*The Discourses*: 300)

DO NOT KEEP MALCONTENTS

In managing, especially in a new organization, you will always find a few people who resist everything you are trying to accomplish. It is dangerous to keep these people around, and it is critical that a method of disposing of them be created. One tactic is to give them the ultimate choice: Do you want to work here or not?

[You either develop soldiers who are successful] by . . . practice of [the Art of War] or by [the] necessity [of protecting themselves] . . . where [they] are constrained either to overcome or die (because [they] can never hope to get [away by fleeing]).

(*The Art of War*: 522)

If they fail to become good soldiers after having been given the choice of improving their performance or leaving the organization, you have no option but to immediately rid yourself of them.

[A]nd if constrained to put any one to death, he should do so only when there is manifest cause or reasonable justification.

(*The Prince*: 121)

Once the decision to fire them has been made, it is always critical to rid them from the organization as soon as possible. This is true even if it is necessary to pay them their salaries for a period of time in order to satisfy employment rules and regulations. Terminated employees who remain within the walls of the organization spread discontent to the remaining workers, and in the extreme they can cause physical damage to you or the organization.

MAKE CHANGES IN A TIMELY MANNER

When you build or acquire a new empire, any redesigns of the organizational or staffing structure should be made immediately. And when you make these changes, you must at the same time design and implement new policies and procedures to complement them. The more drastic the change, the more important it is to perform the acts rapidly. While there may be complaints about your actions and employees may threaten to leave the organization, or may actually leave, it is more advantageous to have all negative acts performed at once, rather than to have constant disruptions. Once you have performed the deeds of change, it is then possible to comfort the employees and staff that remain with benefits. With the passage of time they will forget the changes, and if you have initiated proper policies and procedures, the new will soon become the old.

Whence it is to be noted that in taking a state the conqueror must arrange to commit all his cruelties at once, so as not to have to recur to them every day, and so as to be able, by not making fresh changes, to reassure people and win them over by benefiting them. Whosoever, either through timidity or from following bad counsels, acts otherwise, must keep the sword always drawn, and can put no trust in his subjects, who suffering from continued and constantly renewed severities, can never feel sure of him.

(*The Prince*: 63)

DON'T BE CRUEL

In managing it is okay to be autocratic and it is okay to be a disciplinarian; however, it is never okay to be excessively cruel. As I have said before, if you can have someone else perform whatever cruel acts are necessary, all the better.

Cruel acts are not necessarily evil, and they should never be committed just for the sake of being assertive. Cruel acts should only be used when they are necessary to ensure the success of the organization and your empire. They only carry the label cruel because the consequences of them cause damage to selected individuals.

[C]ruelties . . . are well employed, if it be permitted to speak well of things evil, which are done once for all as necessary for your security, and are not afterwards persisted in, but so far as possible modified to the advantage of the governed. Ill-employed cruelties, on the other hand, are those which from small beginnings increase rather than diminish with time. They who follow the first of these methods, may . . . find . . . that their condition is not desperate; but by no possibility can the others maintain themselves.

(*The Prince*: 62–63)

WHEN IT IS TIME TO DO IT—DO IT

If it becomes necessary to fire or lay off a number of people when initially organizing or in reorganizing an organization, it is best to do it on a single day. If the budget must be cut, then cut it all at once, rather than make additional cuts monthly or quarterly.

Injuries, therefore, should be inflicted all at once, that their ill [taste] being less lasting may less offend; whereas, benefits should be conferred little by little, that so they may be more fully relished. . . . [b]efore all things, a Prince should so live with his subjects that no [change] for better or worse shall cause him to alter his behavior; for if the need to change come through adversity, it is too late to resort to severity; and any leniency you may then use will be thrown away, since it will be seen to be compulsory and bring you no thanks.

(*The Prince*: 63–64).

In laying off people or cutting the budget, it is always better to err on the side of laying off too many or cutting too much. Once the situation is modified and improved, it is always possible to hire more people, and you can always increase the budget in the middle of a budget period if money becomes available. These actions then become favors you can bestow. But if you misjudge a quarterly estimate and must have continual layoffs or impose new budget cuts, you will constantly create new turmoil.

And this turmoil acts as a blockade on your road to success and will shake the foundations of your empire.

[it] does great wrong constantly to excite the resentment of its subjects by fresh injuries to this or that individual [among] them.

(*The Discourses*: 191)

    A manager who attempts to build, acquire, or maintain an empire without loyal staff support is doomed to failure. And just as your staff members owe their loyalty to you, it is of great importance that you reciprocate by giving the proper degree of loyalty and respect to them. And you must always treat them fairly.

20

Things for Which a Manager Is Praised or Blamed

The wish to acquire is no doubt a natural and common sentiment, and when men attempt things within their power, they will always be praised rather than blamed. But when they persist in attempts that are beyond their power, mishaps and blame ensue.

(*The Prince*: 41)

A manager who strives for excellence must do more than read books about excellent companies. It is necessary to eat, drink, and sleep management thoughts and ideas. This does not imply that you work all the time, but it does mean that no matter where you are or what you are doing, you are thinking about the office or plant, and how you can be a better manager.

[Among] other essentials for a general is the knowledge of localities and countries, without which general and particular knowledge he cannot successfully undertake any enterprise. And although the acquirement of every science demands practice, yet to possess this one perfectly requires more than any other.

(*The Discourses*: 417)

While you are engaged in other activities, you should always watch and analyze the acts of workers performing various jobs. There is a management lesson to learn in nearly everything you see. If you go to McDonald's, observe the actions of the workers preparing your order. If you go to a sporting event, watch the actions of the various workers. You should observe how other organizations provide, or fail to provide, good customer service and how they advertise their products or services. Your thought should constantly be about how to be the best.

MANAGE APPROPRIATELY

The world of organizations is far from perfect, and there are those with whom you will come into contact who are ruthless for the sake of being ruthless. Therefore, it is important to learn how to manage appropriately. Don't just manage, manage the situation.

It is essential, therefore, for a Prince who would maintain his position, to have learned how to be other than good, and to use or not to use his goodness as necessity requires.

(The Prince: 110)

There is neither the perfect worker nor the perfect manager, but this does not mean that you should not strive to be not only the best manager in your organization, but also the best manager who has ever been. However, do not disparage yourself if you do not always perform at your best.

[S]ince anyone who would . . . [be perfect] in everything, must be ruined among so many who are not good.

(The Prince: 110)

BLAME IS LEGION

At times it may seem that you are being constantly blamed not only for things you are responsible for, but for things that you do not even have control over.

Good managers are blamed in various degrees and at various times for going over budget. Strive to keep within your budget, unless you can show positive results from going over budget or can go over budget without being detected.

Managers are blamed if they recruit people in the organization who do not conform to the corporate culture. Therefore, use caution in your recruiting.

Managers are blamed for having excessive perks; therefore you should abstain from conspicuous consumption and enjoy the rewards of being a successful manager in a subdued manner.

Managers are blamed for being stingy with raises to their staffs. Therefore be generous with raises when your staff is worthy. When you are rewarded for the performance of your organization, assure that your staff shares in that reward.

And although an [organization] may be poor and able to give but little, yet she should not abstain from giving that little; for even the smallest reward for a good action—no matter how important the service to the [organization]—will always be esteemed by the recipient as most honorable.

(The Discourses: 153–54)

Managers are blamed for making organizational changes. However, by following the advice I have previously given, you can learn to make changes effectively and efficiently, and you should never let the fact that you might be blamed or despised for making the changes a reason for avoiding change.

Managers are blamed for disciplining their staffs and firing or laying off staff members. However, these actions are often a necessity and are part of the job of being a manager.

Managers are blamed for being grouchy from time to time; therefore when your moods are less than friendly, you should insulate yourself from staff members until you can display a cheerful attitude.

One of the many other causes for blame is filing expenses or performance reports after their due date; therefore the wise manager is timely in filing all of his reports.

Much of the blame a manager receives can be traced to his own actions or inactions, often committed at times when he knew it was probably wrong or unwise to do or not do them.

And yet nearly all men, deceived by a false good and a false glory, allow themselves voluntarily or ignorantly to be drawn towards those who deserve more blame than praise.

(The Discourses: 123)

Blame can also come from outside the organization, from customers disappointed with the services rendered or from government agencies displeased with things a manager does or does not do.

The manager who is trying to be the best often receives blame from his family. This may be the toughest blame for the manager to bear. This blame is usually for working too hard and being away from home too often. If you are to be a true success you must measure these situations carefully and realize that the most successful managers—and those who have long tenure in organizations—are those who can maintain both an active work life and a happy home life.

PRAISE IS RARE

It is a maxim that managers are praised less often than they are blamed. If praise is what you need for happiness or for personal satisfaction, then you should consider being something besides a manager.

And there are none so foolish or so wise, so wicked or so good, that, in choosing between these [good and wicked managers], they do not praise what is praise-worthy and blame that which deserves blame.

(The Discourses: 123)

The best praises and the ones that you will most often receive are your own, your self-appraisals of how you are doing. Do not be afraid to pat yourself on the back. It is as important to give yourself internal self-praise—and self-blame when appropriate—as it is to receive it from others.

Occasionally managers are praised for achieving the goals of the organization, including sales and other performance measurements. They are also praised for bringing new customers to the organization, increasing their own educational level, or being involved in community organizations and being generous in volunteering their time to community endeavors.

Often a manager cannot avoid blame; nor do his actions, even though worthy, always result in praise. This is the lot of the managing class. A wise manager should judge his virtue not by what others say, but rather by his own standards.

ONLY THE STRONG SURVIVE

Managers also need to be tough in personality, because they often are blamed for things they have not done. If this happens you should not let rumors or unjust criticism alter your behavior or motives. What you should do is to evaluate the nature and purpose of the criticism and modify your actions only where it is appropriate.

But he need never hesitate to incur the reproach of those vices without which his authority can hardly be preserved; for if he well consider the whole matter, he will find that there may be a line of conduct having the appearance of virtue . . . [that if followed] would be his ruin, and that there may be another course having the appearance of vice, by following which his safety and well-being are secured.

(The Prince: 111–12)

21
Truth

[A] Prince should know how to use the beast's nature wisely, he ought of beasts to choose both the lion and the fox; for the lion cannot guard himself from the [traps], nor the fox from wolves. He must therefore be a fox to discern [traps], and a lion to drive off wolves. To rely wholly on the lion is unwise; and for this reason a prudent Prince neither can nor ought to keep his word when to keep it is hurtful to him and the causes which led him to pledge it are removed.

(*The Prince*: 126)

Truth is an important characteristic of a wise manager. And if you are to be successful and gain and keep power, you must have a clear understanding of the nature and purpose of truth. Above all, a manager must always hear the truth from those who act as advisors and assistants. You can only know what is really happening in an organization, what the problems are, and what actions to take if those you have selected as advisors tell you the whole truth about organizational matters.

SEEK THE TRUTH

You won't learn the truth unless you want to know it. This trait of wanting to know the truth is a quality that separates the great managers from the average. Most managers want only good news and want only to receive flattery.

[B]ecause men take so much pleasure in their own concerns, and so deceive themselves with regard to them . . . they can hardly escape . . . [the plague of flattery]; while even in the effort to escape it there is risk of incurring contempt. For there is no way to guard against flattery but by letting it be seen that you take no offense in hearing the truth: but when every one is free to tell you the truth, respect falls short.

(*The Prince*: 174–75)

It is important to select only a few advisors. And after their selection, assure them through your conduct and actions that no harm will come to them from speaking the truth. Should you violate this rule with any of them, then out of their own self-interest your other advisors will no longer tell you the entire truth. Hiding from reality either through choice or through the actions of others can destroy you faster than any other thing you might do.

[A] prudent Prince should [choose] certain discreet men from among his sub-jects, and [allow] them alone [freedom] to speak their minds on any matter on which he asks their opinion, and on none other. But he ought to ask their opin-ion on everything, and after hearing what they have to say, should reflect and judge for himself. And with these counsellors collectively, and with each of them separately, his bearing should be such, that each and all of them may know that the more freely they speak their minds the better they will be liked. Besides these, the Prince should listen to no others, but should follow the course determined, and afterwards adhere firmly to his resolves. Whoever acts otherwise is either undone by flatterers, or, from continually vacillating as opinions vary, comes to be held in light esteem.

(*The Prince*: 175)

HEAR THE TRUTH

When asking for the truth you should select the moments when you want to hear it, but you should want to hear it often.

A Prince, therefore, ought always to take counsel, but at such times and seasons only as he himself pleases, and not when it pleases others; . . . [he] should discourage every one from . . . [offering] advice on matters on which it is not sought. But he should be free in asking advice, and afterwards, as regards the matters on which he has asked it, a patient hearer of the truth, and even [be] displeased should he perceive that any one, from whatsoever motive, keeps it back.

(*The Prince*: 176–77).

TELL THE TRUTH

Not only is it important to hear the truth, but it is important—most of the time—to tell the truth. Indeed, it should be the goal of every manager to tell the truth all of the time. However, because your subordinates, superiors, and opponents do not tell the truth, you must manipulate the truth if it becomes necessary for your survival. Because the truth is so important, this is perhaps the hardest advice to give a manager.

If all men were good, this would not be good advice, but since they are dishonest and do not keep faith with you, you, in return, need not keep faith with them.
(*The Prince*: 126–27)

The truth or a lie can also be told by a manager through his silence. This fact is not only helpful in learning how not to let your silence speak for you, but in learning to interpret what silence from others really means when you are asking questions of them. This silence is known as tacit confession, and it is guilt that is acknowledged by total silence or delayed denial. It is telling the truth or not telling the truth through silence. When being questioned about things you would rather not talk about, it is important that you learn to deny any action immediately without hesitation. Don't let your silence speak for you, and don't let your hesitation in denial be a confession to the real truth. If you find it necessary to lie, then you need to learn how to lie instantly.

DEALING WITH SLANDER

It is harmful to you when those you rely on fail to tell you the truth, especially if they are making an accusation against someone by inference. And when you discover that advisors or subordinates have failed to tell the whole truth, or have spread dissent among those who attempted to tell you the truth, you should deal with these advisors or subordinates in a just and fair but firm manner.

[He] was a calumniator, and not an accuser; and the Romans showed in his case how calumniators ought to be punished. For they ought to be made to be accusers; and, if the accusation proves true, they should be rewarded, or at least not punished; but if it proves not to be true, then they should be punished
(*The Discourses*: 119–20)

AVOIDING A LIE

If you conduct your affairs properly—limit those who have access to advise you—you will rarely have to tell a total lie. And you may avoid the need to lie at all by making plausible explanations or mental reservations for your actions, and by relying on constructive denial of ambiguous facts.

It is often wise to have close advisors keep minor details of a situation from you. This can spare you from the necessity of knowing the whole truth. What you don't know you can't lie about. This does not violate the principle that they should tell you the whole truth, because you have an understanding with them that the information they withhold is not damaging to your decision making. The goal is to provide you with plausible deniability.

However, if they tell you something you don't want to hear and you try to avoid it by saying, "I don't want to know," in fact you can no longer plausibly deny it. You can only lie. And in this case, only you can be the judge of the harm in following this course of action.

CHANGING CIRCUMSTANCES

In the course of managing, circumstances change and things you have said or promised can be modified without outright lying. Contracts can be broken, agreements modified, punishments inflicted, and benefits withheld. However, you should keep in mind that this principle might be invoked by other managers you are dealing with; therefore, when you want an ironclad agreement, make sure it contains as few loopholes as possible or at least that the loopholes only apply to you.

[No] Prince was ever at a loss for plausible reasons to cloak a breach of faith. . . . It is necessary, indeed, to put a good color on acts of this nature, and to be skilful in feigning and dissembling. But men are so simple, and governed so absolutely by their present needs, that he who wishes to deceive will never fail in finding willing dupes.

(*The Prince*: 127)

The best course of action I can advise a manager to follow is to tell the truth and to assure himself, because it is vital, that his advisors and assistants do likewise. But he should constantly be on the lookout for those who do not.

Every one recognizes how praiseworthy it is for a Prince to keep faith, and to act uprightly and craftily. Nevertheless . . . [there have been] Princes who have set little store by their word, but have known how to overreach others by their cunning, have accomplished great things, and in the end had the better of those who trusted to honest dealing.

(*The Prince*: 125)

22
Things to Avoid

[A] Prince . . . should consider how he may avoid such courses as would make him hated or despised; and that whenever he succeeds in keeping clear of these, he has performed his part, and runs no risk though he incur other reproaches. . . . [He more readily] becomes hated by being . . . [excessively greedy] and by interfering with the . . . [benefits] of his subjects, than in any other way. From [this], therefore, he should abstain. For so long as . . . [neither their benefits] nor their honor is touched, the mass of mankind live contentedly, and the Prince has only to cope with the ambition of a few, which can in many ways and easily be kept within bounds.

(*The Prince*: 131–32)

Machiavelli said it very clearly: above all things, avoid being hated.

BE RESPECTED

People may disagree with you, they may not like your company or they may not want to play golf with you, but if you are honorable and consistent in seeking your goals you will receive respect.

And if you have respect from your superiors, other managers, and your subordinates, you will fare well in the achievement of your goals. But this respect is not given to the weak manager, but rather to the strong. Without it, you are doomed to being constantly faced with conflict situations. All managers are sometimes faced with conflict, however, and when this happens, in order to be a successful manager you must confront it openly and never back down.

[N]o prince should ever forego his rank, nor should he ever voluntarily give up anything (wishing to do so honorably) unless he is able or believes himself able to hold it. For it is almost always better (matters having come to the point that he cannot give it up in the above manner) to allow it to be taken from him by force, rather than by the apprehension of force. For if he yields it from fear, it is for the purpose of avoiding war, and he will rarely escape from that; for he to whom he has from cowardice conceded the one thing will not be satisfied, but will want to take other things from him, and his arrogance will increase as his esteem for the prince is lessened. And, on the other hand, the zeal of the prince's friends will be chilled on seeing him appear feeble or cowardly. But if, so soon as he discerns his adversary's intention, he prepares his forces, even though they be inferior, the enemy will begin to respect him, and the other neighboring princes will appreciate him the more; and seeing him armed for defense, those even will come to his aid who, seeing him give up himself, would never have assisted him. This reasoning applies to the case when there is only one enemy; but when there are several, it will always be a wise plan for the prince to yield something of his possessions to some one of them, either for the purpose of gaining him over if war has already been declared, or to detach him from the enemies that are leagued against him.

(*The Discourses*: 261–62)

Let Your Decisions Be Final

Do not be "wishy-washy." When you make a decision, stick with it. Make changes only when it is to your advantage to do so. Be generous with your staff, favoring them with the things that please them, as long as this does not disrupt the organization. Be considerate and kind to your secretary and advisors.

A Prince is despised when he is seen to be fickle, frivolous, effeminate, . . . [cowardly], or irresolute, against which defects he ought therefore to guard most carefully, striving so to bear himself that greatness, courage, wisdom, and strength may appear in all his actions. In his private dealings with his subjects his decisions should be irrevocable, and his reputation such that no one would dream of overreaching or cajoling him.

(*The Prince*: 132)

Be Yourself

And since you cannot be all things to all employees, be yourself. In selecting a style of management, the one thing a manager must avoid is saying that he believes in one course of action, and then in his actions and conduct showing that in truth he believes in the opposite. The manager who acts in this manner is a fraud, and of all the management types, this is the most detestable.

Avoid Spreading Rumors

The lawgiver of a republic . . . should give every citizen the right to accuse another citizen without fear or suspicion; and this being done, and properly carried out, he should severely punish calumniators, who would have no right to complain of such punishment, it being open to them to bring charges against those whom they had in private calumniated. And where this system is not well established there will always be great disorders, for calumnies irritate, but do not chastise men; and those who have been thus irritated will think of [revenging] themselves, hating more than fearing the slanders spread against them.

(The Discourses: 118)

Avoid Fooling Around

A wise manager should never fool around with his secretary or with his subordinates, and this is true for both genders of managers. Of all the actions that can cost you your position, this one can cause the most irreparable damage. And while this is true for all managers, it is absolutely true for managers who are married. A manager who cheats on his spouse can hardly expect to be trusted by superiors, subordinates, or customers. They will make the observation that if you cheat on your spouse you will certainly cheat them.

Avoid Scandal or the Appearance of Scandal

A manager should avoid scandal or the appearance of scandal. You should not always let your virtue be judged by others, but rather by what you know to be true. Be concerned about rumors, but always use caution in modifying your behavior because of untrue rumors. Doing this can make you look guilty when you are not.

[H]e must be discreet enough to know how to avoid the reproach of those vices that would deprive him of his [organization], and, if possible, be on his guard also against those which might not deprive him of it; though if he cannot wholly restrain himself, he may with less scruple indulge in the latter.

(The Prince: 111)

Be firm in your actions, perform noble acts, and care about others.

The Prince who inspires such an opinion of himself is greatly esteemed, and against one who is greatly esteemed conspiracy is difficult, nor , when he is known to be an excellent Prince and held in reverence by his subjects, will it be easy to attack him.

(The Prince: 132)

Respect Your Opponents

Never talk disparagingly about either opponents or allies, superiors or subordinates, or clients or customers. Such talk is unbecoming and causes others to be disrespectful of you. Speaking in such a manner to an opponent it will only cause him to oppose you with more vigor. And when people hear you talk in this manner about others, they will believe that you also talk so about them, and this leads to suspicion and distrust.

It is the duty . . . of every good general of an army, or chief of a republic, to use all proper means to prevent such insults and reproaches from being indulged in by citizens or soldiers, either among themselves or against the enemy; for if used against an enemy they give rise [to their increased anger and resolve in defeating you], and between the soldiers and the citizens it is even worse, unless they are promptly put a stop to, as has [always] been done by prudent rulers.

(The Discourses: 301-2)

[B]ecause nothing is more irritating and calculated to excite greater indignation than such reproaches, whether founded upon truth or not; ''for harsh sarcasms, even if they have but the least truth in them, leave their bitterness rankling in the memory.''

(The Discourses: 302)

Keep Your Fears in Perspective

A manager's fears can be divided into two categories. You are either afraid that an opponent inside your organization will attack you, or you are afraid of attack from outside your organization.

For a Prince is exposed to two dangers, from within in respect of his subjects, from without in respect of foreign powers. Against the latter he will defend himself with good arms and good allies, and if he [has] good arms he will always have good allies; and when things are settled . . . [externally], they will always be settled at home, unless disturbed by conspiracies; and even should there be hostility from without, if he has taken those measures, and has lived in the way I have recommended, and if he never despairs, he will withstand every attack.

(The Prince: 132-33)

Do Not Disclose Secret Intentions

Avoid showing others any discontent you have about the organization. Keep your complaints to yourself. Any plans you have for acquiring other organizations keep to yourself, or only discuss them with those few you determine are your true friends, those with whom you can discuss anything. If your intentions are to take corrective action, or you intend to oppose someone, don't tell that person or others what you are going to do. Wait, and when the deed is done, they will know.

From this we plainly see the folly and imprudence of demanding a thing, and saying beforehand that it is intended to be used for evil; . . . and one should never show one's intentions, but endeavor to obtain one's desires anyhow. For it is enough to ask a man to give up his arms, without telling him that you intend killing him with them; after you have the arms in hand, then you can do your will with them.

(*The Discourses*: 190)

Avoid Conspiracies

Conspiracies are dangerous to a manager not only when he is their victim, but also when he is a participant.

[F]or history teaches us that many more princes have lost their lives and their states by conspiracies than by open war. But few can venture to make open war upon their sovereign, [while] everyone may engage in conspiracies against him. On the other hand, subjects cannot undertake more perilous and foolhardy enterprises than conspiracies, which are in every respect most difficult and dangerous; and [so] it is that, though so often attempted, yet they so rarely attain the desired object.

(*The Discourses*: 329)

Therefore you should avoid being involved in conspiracies. If you find the need to engage in a plot, you should do so only by yourself.

A plot may be formed by a single individual or by many; the one cannot be called a conspiracy, but rather a determined purpose on the part of one man. . . . In such case the first of the three dangers to which conspiracies are exposed is avoided; for the individual runs no risk before the execution of his plot, for as not one possesses his secret, there is no danger of his purpose coming to the ears of [another].

(*The Discourses*: 331)

If you must conspire, keep the number of co-conspirators as small as possible, preferably to no more than one. Almost everyone will tell your secret, even though spoken in darkness, when it is in the teller's best interest and will give him protection—as you would tell his.

One should therefore never open himself on the subject of a conspiracy except under the most pressing necessity, and only at the moment of its execution; and then only to one man, whose fidelity he has thoroughly tested for a long time, and who is animated by the same desire as himself. One such is much more easily found than many, and therefore there is much less danger in confiding your secret to him; and then even if he were to attempt to betray you, there is some chance of your being able to defend yourself, which you cannot when there are many conspirators.

(The Discourses: 337)

Never conspire through letters or memoranda.

You may escape, then, from the accusation of a single individual, unless you are convicted by some writing or other pledge, which you should be careful never to give.

(The Discourses: 338)

If a person attempts a conspiracy against you, it is usually because he believes that he will satisfy others by destroying you. But if it appears that your superiors, subordinates, or other managers will be offended, and perhaps seek justice, by your destruction, then conspiring against you becomes too dangerous. There are only a few who give no thought for themselves, either through ignorance or by being misguided by others. While rare, these are always dangerous and should be avoided and when possible destroyed.

[D]eaths like this which are the result of a deliberate and fixed resolve, cannot be escaped by Princes, since any one who disregards his own life can effect them. A Prince, however, needs the less to fear them as they are seldom attempted.
(The Prince: 146)

Conspiracies can be avoided if you conduct yourself in the manner I have prescribed, avoid being hated by the majority, and do not drive others to desperation.

[A manager] has little to fear from conspiracies when his subjects are well a fected towards him; but when they are hostile and hold him in abhorrence, he he s then reason to fear everything and everyone. And well ordered [organizatior s] and wise [managers] have provided with extreme care that the nobility shall not be driven to desperation, and that the commons shall be kept satisfied and contented; for this is one of the most important matters that a [manager] has to look to.
(The Prince: 136)

Do Not Put Secrets in Writing

When a secret intention is in your handwriting it becomes difficult to deny it—although of course you should. And in today's world the same holds true if it is on audio or video tape. The best place to tell secrets is in the middle of an open field away from buildings and trees. And then, of course, as I have said, telling anyone is hazardous.

[A]nd therefore one should guard most carefully against writing, as against a dangerous rock, for nothing will convict you quicker than your own handwriting.

(*The Discourses*: 338)

Avoid Sex with Others in Your Organization

In today's world this warning is applicable to both genders:

[W]e see that women have been the cause of great dissensions and much ruin to states, and have caused great damage to those who govern them.

(*The Discourses*: 390–91)

Avoid Malcontents

[As] soon as you impart your design to a discontented man, you supply him with the means of removing his discontent, since by betraying you he can procure for himself every advantage; so that seeing on the one hand certain gain, and on the other a doubtful and dangerous risk, he must either be a rare friend to you, or the mortal enemy of the Prince, if he [keeps] your secret.

(*The Prince*: 134)

Avoid the Appearance of Greed

But the ambition of men is such that to gratify a present desire, they think not of the evils which will in a short time result from it.

(*The Discourses*: 284)

Avoid Unprofitable Alliances

Don't make alliances with those more powerful than you.

[A] Prince should be careful never to join with one stronger than himself in attacking others, unless, as already said, he be driven to it by necessity. For if he whom you join with prevails, you are at his mercy; and Princes, so far as in them lies, should avoid placing themselves at the mercy of others.

(*The Prince*: 168)

Avoid Making Threats

[A] proof of great prudence for men [is] to abstain from threats and insulting words towards any one, for neither the one nor the other in any way diminishes the strength of the enemy; but the one makes him more cautious, and the other increases his hatred of you, and makes him more persevering in his efforts to injure you.

(*The Discourses*: 301)

Avoid Mistreating Advisors and Assistants

Remember that advisors and assistants are the source of your strength and the protectors of your power.

Avoid Familiarity

Avoid familiarity with subordinate persons in the organization. Familiarity not only breeds contempt but carries with it the seeds of discontent. Subordinates perform more effectively and efficiently for managers who are thought to be special. And a manager becomes special who is perceived to have unknown qualities. If subordinates become too familiar with you, the mystique will be broken and they will no longer think you special.

A FINAL WARNING

While a complete list of things to avoid is impossible to compile, the best advise I can give you is to use your judgment in deciding whether to avoid a particular action. Generally, if it is necessary for you to consider avoiding it, the answer is yes, avoid it.

If you heed the warnings in this chapter and conduct yourself in a proper manner, you will become more successful and also not be an object of hatred and contempt; and as I have said, above all things you must avoid being hated.

23

Avoiding Flattery

[B]ecause men take so much pleasure in their own concerns, and so
deceive themselves with regard to them, that they can hardly
escape . . . [the plague of flattery]; while even in the effort to escape
it there is risk of incurring contempt.

(The Prince: 174)

Even though you may be the best in your organization—or on the way
to being the best—you must never outwardly behave as if entitled to be
called the best. And you should never let your belief that you are the
best cause you to quit trying to be better. On your road to success and
excellence, it is important that your attitude always be one that drives
your desire to work hard and achieve more than anyone else in the
organization. Indeed, this attitude is critical if you are to reach your goals
and realize your full potential. This is true whether you are a front-line
supervisor of a small company or the president of a multinational
organization. The further up the ladder you are, the further you can fall.
History is full of examples of princes and managers who have fallen from
the highest summit to the lowest pit.

DO NOT ALWAYS BELIEVE YOUR PRESS

One thing that causes top achievers to start feeling that they have
reached their summit and may now quit trying to be better is that they

begin to believe their own positive press, or disbelieve their negative press. When people say they are doing a great job or are working hard, they begin to think they have done enough. They quit trying and let their guard down. And when this happens the opposition quickly steps in to grab their power.

[F]or when one has judgment to discern the good from the bad in what another says or does, though he be devoid of invention, he can recognize the merits and demerits of his servant, and will commend the former while he corrects the latter. The servant cannot hope to deceive such a master, and will continue good.

(*The Prince*: 172)

ACQUIRE APPROPRIATE HUMILITY

A wise manager is always on guard against potentially adverse times. He understands that no one likes people who seem to be overly self-assured and do not express a degree of humility.

[A] multitude is more easily governed by humanity and gentleness than by haughtiness and cruelty.

(*The Discourses*: 376)

Therefore, if you are to be wise you should develop a posture of humility and not be ostentatious in your actions.

SELECT WISE ADVISORS

A manager is never successful only because of his advisors. He shows his merit by selecting wise advisors, retaining them, and listening to them.

[I]t is an unerring rule and of universal application that a Prince who is not wise himself cannot be well advised by others, unless by chance he surrender himself to be wholly governed by some one adviser who happens to be supremely prudent; in which case he may, indeed, be well advised; but not for long, since such an adviser will soon oust him from his Princedom. If he listens to a multitude of advisers, the Prince who is not wise will never have consistent counsels, nor will he know . . . how to reconcile them. Each of his counsellors will study his own advantage, and the Prince will be unable to detect or correct them. Nor could it well be otherwise, for men will always [be false to you] unless they find themselves under a necessity to be honest. We may take it therefore that good counsels [from wherever] they come, have their origin in the prudence of the Prince, and not the prudence of the Prince in wise counsels.

(*The Prince*: 177–78)

24

Fortune

I would liken her to one of those wild torrents which, when angry, overflow the plains, sweep away trees and houses, and carry off soil from one bank to throw it down upon the other. Everyone flees before them, and yields to their fury without the least power to resist. And yet, though this be their nature, it does not follow that in seasons of fair weather, men cannot, by constructing . . . [dikes and banks], make such provision as will cause them when again in flood to pass off by some artificial channel, or at least prevent their course from being so uncontrolled and destructive. And so it is with Fortune, who displays her might where there is no prepared strength to resist her, and directs her onset where she knows there is neither barrier nor embankment to confine her.

(*The Prince*: 184)

Luck and fortune govern events that happen daily but cannot be explained through normal reasoning. Incidents of this type occur constantly in every organization and to every manager.

However, luck is often only an excuse a manager uses to describe the successes of others over his own failures. While the manager may find comfort in this, he will never find success. You should never blame luck for your own failures. It is more beneficial to accept a failure as a learning experience, and not excuse it away. Experience is like a ladder; you can either climb up to success and victory, or further down to failure and defeat.

CAPITALIZE ON OTHERS' FAILURES

The failures of others can prove beneficial to you. And it is important that you learn to capitalize on these failures, but you can only do so if you are prepared. Therefore, to reach success you should define those events that others call luck as just events that happen, and capitalize on them by being prepared to grasp the opportunities when they are presented.

[F]or as some men desire to have more, [while] others fear to lose what they have, enmities and war are the consequences; and this brings about the ruin of one province and the elevation of another.

(*The Discourses*: 174)

PURSUE LUCK

What luck and fortune there may be can only be capitalized on if you pursue it aggressively. And this pursuit begins when you begin planning, setting goals, and preparing yourself for the future.

[T]he [manager] who rests wholly on Fortune is ruined when she changes. . . . [H]e will prosper most whose mode of acting best adapts itself to the character of the times; and conversely . . . he will be unprosperous, with whose mode of acting the times do not accord. For we see that men in those matters which lead to the end each has before him, namely, glory and wealth, proceed by different ways, one with caution, another with impetuosity, one with violence, another with subtlety, one with patience, another with its contrary; and that by one or other of these different courses each may succeed.

Again, of two who act cautiously, you . . . find that one attains his end, the other not, and that two different temperaments, the one cautious, the other impetuous, are alike successful. All which happens from no other cause than that the character of the times accords or does not accord with their method of acting. And hence it comes . . . that two operating differently arrive at the same result and two operating similarly, the one succeeds, the other not.

(*The Prince*: 185–86)

However, luck does not stand alone. When you examine those who appear to be lucky you will find that mingled with their luck is also excellence, power, and prudence. So you should be virtuous and prudent in all your actions.

Luck, fortune, destiny, divine will—whatever they may be and by whatever name they are called—can only benefit you if you are prepared when they present themselves. It is necessary if you want to be successful never to depend on them alone. You must constantly enhance your management education, and you must constantly practice both the science and art of management. For to be successful you need not know the exact reasons why things happen that appear to be lucky; you need only be prepared, so that when opportunity knocks, you are ready to answer.

25
Change

And this rule should be observed by all who wish to abolish an existing system of government in any state, and introduce a new and more liberal one. For as all [change] excite the minds of men, it is important to retain in such innovations as much as possible the previously existing forms. And if the number, authority, and duration of the term of service of the magistrates be changed, the titles at least ought to be preserved.

(The Discourses: 155)

It is a maxim that change is necessary and inevitable. For growth, it is necessary that an organization change both consistently and constantly. Any organization that does not change with the times is a prime candidate for takeover by another organization. This is true whether it be a department being taken over by another department or a company being acquired by another company. Or if a takeover does not occur, then the inflexible organization will self-destruct, because it will allow another organization to capture its market.

FAILURE TO CHANGE BRINGS DESTRUCTION

The same is true for managers. If they do not change with the times they too will be destroyed, and in the process they will destroy those around them. Even a manager who appears to survive by clinging to past methods of operation and refusing to accept new technology and new procedures is partly destroyed, because that manager never achieved what could have been achieved by accepting change.

A senior manager or CEO who allows lower-level managers who refuse to change to remain in his organization because it is less disruptive, is helping to destroy the organization. In such a case the senior manager is a failure to himself, to the owners of the organization, and to the employees and staff. Everyone suffers because of his neglect in forcing change. These managers and organizations will be attacked by corporate raiders or internal opponents and will become not the victors but the losers.

THE BIG PICTURE—AGAIN

Capitalism has only been successful because of its ability to modify itself and change with the times. If the capitalist organizations of the seventeenth and eighteenth centuries had been static in their nature, the gloomy predications of Karl Marx might have come true. Any organization of the latter part of the twentieth century that refuses to modify itself to the times and remains static to the needs of employees and customers is subject to a passive, and possibly an active, revolution against it. And if you as a manager fail to change, your future will also be clouded. You must not take yourself out of the big picture.

There is nothing more true than that all the things of this world have a limit to their existence; but those only run the entire course . . . that do not allow their [structure] to become disorganized, but keep it unchanged in the manner ordained, or if they change it, so do it that it shall be for their advantage, and not to their injury. . . . And those are the best-constituted [organizations], and have the longest existence, which possess the intrinsic means of frequently renewing themselves, or such as obtain this renovation in consequence of some extrinsic accidents. And it is a truth clearer than light that, without such renovations, these [organizations] cannot continue to exist; and the means of renewing them is to bring them back to their original principles.

(*The Discourses*: 319)

STARTING OVER

Every organization must be willing to face the future as if it were starting anew. And when managers plan for themselves and their organizations, they must approach the planning process not only as a continuation of their previous plans, but as an opportunity to chart a new course for the future. They must be willing to plow up old fields in order to plant new crops, so as to harvest new opportunities. You as a manager must look into the future without measuring and being bounded by the past. And not only must you accept inevitable change, but you must develop an attitude of wanting to change. It is this positive attitude toward change that separates average managers from superstar managers.

CHANGING YOUR CHARACTER

However, when you as a manager are changing your character or your style or management, you should not do it rapidly, but slowly in stages.

For he who for a time has seemed good, and for purposes of his own wants to become bad, should do it gradually, and should seem to be brought to it by the force of circumstances; so that, before his changed nature deprives him of his former friends, he may have gained new ones, and that his authority may not be diminished by the change. Otherwise his deception will be discovered, and he will lose his friends and be ruined.

(The Discourses: 187)

MAKING STRUCTURAL CHANGES

Most structural changes within an organization, especially when they are major and necessitated by structural flaws, should most often be made immediately and completely. Even though this is difficult to accomplish, a wise manager makes plans that will accommodate unforeseen changes.

[Once the structure of an organization] has been discovered to be no longer suitable, [it] should be amended, either all at once, or by degrees as each defect becomes known . . . [and] both of these courses are equally impossible. For a gradual modification requires to be the work of some wise man, who has seen the evil from afar in its very beginning.

(The Discourses: 145)

CHANGE IS DIFFICULT

For change to be rapid and effective, it must come from the few and not the many, from the exceptional manager and not the average. However, in your striving for excellence, for success, and for power, you will find most often that change is difficult to implement. Indeed, it is the most challenging endeavor you face. Those who will be inconvenienced and those who fear that they will lose some benefit of their positions, will resist change at every juncture.

[B]ut it is very likely that such a man may never rise up in the state, and even if he did he will hardly be able to persuade the others to what he proposes; for men accustomed to live after one fashion do not like to change, and the less so as they do not see the evil staring them in the face, but presented to them as a mere conjecture.

(The Discourses: 145)

OVERCOMING RESISTANCE TO CHANGE

A cardinal principle of change is that there is a direct relationship between the amount of change that is being attempted and the resistance people will make to that change. As the amount of change increases, the resistance to it also increases. And most often that increase in resistance is geometric, not linear. Therefore the more change you attempt, the more problems will arise. Indeed, everything you try to accomplish finds its roots in change.

FINISH WHAT YOU START

Once you begin the process of change, it is important to complete what you have started. Half-change or incomplete change can be worse than no change at all.

CHANGE EVERYTHING

Often when managers think problems within an organization can be fixed by only changing policy, it is really total change of the organization that is necessary. Almost every change in structure must be accompanied by change in policy, and one without the other is usually counterproductive. However, to fine-tune the organization, minor changes can be made in either structure or policy without affecting the other. For the most part, changes in structure should equal changes in policies and procedures.

THE GOAL OF CHANGE

The goal of change, and it should become your goal of change, is not to keep your organization as it is but to make it different. The goal must be to develop an organization that is not overwhelmed by the changes it is confronted with but can meet the challenges of a changing world. It is not enough to establish a state of change; you must also create a status quo that is itself constantly changing, constantly seeking new and better methods of meeting the challenges of change. This attitude or state of change is called inchoate change, because the new change becomes the old, which is in itself change.

[Structure and policies] established in an [organization] at its very origin, when men were still pure, no longer suit when men have become corrupt and bad. And although the [policies] may be changed according to circumstances and events, yet it is seldom or never that the [structure] itself is changed; and for this reason the new [policies] do not suffice, for they are not in harmony with the [structure], that has remained intact.

(The Discourses: 143)

REALLY BIG CHANGE

Major change is accomplished not through the ordinary actions of a manager but through the extraordinary ones. And to successfully accomplish extraordinary change, it takes an extraordinary manager.

As to reforming [organizations] all at once, when their defects have become manifest to everybody, that also is most difficult; for to do this ordinary means will not suffice; they may even be injurious under such circumstances, and therefore it becomes necessary to resort to extraordinary measures, such as violence and arms, and above all things to make one's self absolute master of the state, so as to be able to dispose of it at will.

(The Discourses: 145)

COMPLETED CHANGE

Change is complete when employees and staff members speak of the new policies and procedures as always having been in place, as being "the way we have always done it." This complete change is called quantum change. It is the establishing of an environment in which employees conduct their affairs without referring to policies because their actions reflect the desires of management.

If you are to be successful and wise, you should be motivated by the challenge of change, and as you gain power you will be able to effect change more efficiently. It takes both practice and perseverance to be a true agent of change.

26
Challenges for the Future

[W]hen one prince wishes to obtain something from another, he must not, when the occasion permits, give him time for deliberation. But he must act so as to make the other see the necessity of prompt decision, and that a refusal or delay may cause an immediate and dangerous indignation.

(The Discourses: 424)

Once you have decided that your goal is to be the best manager you can be, it is necessary to make not only a commitment to action but a plan of action. All wise and powerful managers are dynamic goal setters and work actively to seek their goals' realization.

Acting in this like the skilful archer, who seeing that the object he would hit is distant, and knowing the range of his bow, takes aim much above the destined mark; not designing that his arrow should strike so high, but that flying high it may alight at the point intended.

(The Prince: 31–32)

In setting your goals it is very important that they be written, contain the specific actions that need to be taken in order to achieve them, and be capable of being measured. It is not enough to say that you want to be the best, without making a plan for getting there. It is not enough to say you want to improve, without stating what you are going to do to improve, how you are going to do it, and how you will know when you have improved.

BEGIN YOUR FUTURE NOW

If your education is lacking, the time for enrolling in classes is now, not next week. If you don't have a commitment to community service, the time to get involved is now, not next month. If you are not working enough hours at your job, the time to start working more is now, not next quarter. If your organization needs changing, the time to make changes is now, not at some unspecified date in the future.

But it is the worst fault of [weak managers and organizations] to be irresolute, so that whatever part they take is dictated by force; and if any good results from it, it is caused less by their [wisdom] than by necessity.

(The Discourses: 178–79).

If you are to be a successful manager, then you must make choices that will control your destiny. And as I have shown, you use luck as an ally, are prepared for opportunities, and seize them when they arrive.

It is not easy to become a successful manager. The road is long and winding. To follow all the precepts in this book is difficult, because they are not simply rules that you can apply without thought, or are they mere words that you can repeat from which some kind of magical action will suddenly take place. In order for them to be effective, action is demanded. And that action must be yours; no one can act for you. You will never be the best just because someone else wants you to be.

The sea has been divided; the cloud has attended you on your way; the rock has flowed with water; the manna has rained from heaven; everything has concurred to promote your greatness. What remains to be done must be done by you; since not to deprive us of our free will and such share of glory as belongs to us, God will not do everything himself.

(The Prince: 193)

Not only do the precepts and maxims demand action on your part, but they demand thought. Indeed, many of the maxims are incongruent and if put into practice simultaneously can prove counterproductive. The correct principle must be used in the proper situation at the right time. If the wrong principle is selected, or if the right one is used at the wrong time or in the wrong situation, the results to you can be fatal. In fact, some principles become wrong when you use them at the wrong time. Their application is more artistic than scientific. Therefore, it is the uncommon—the extraordinary—manager who can select and compose them in a logical manner, a manner that results in a symphony of successes, not a cacophony of failures.

THE BEGINNING

This guidebook provides you with beginning points that must be carefully studied and analyzed. There is no constant formula, no magic recipe to power and success, because it is your actions that are the key ingredients. You now have all the other ingredients, the tools and techniques. You must decide how to mix them with your life, your goals, and your organization so that they produce the results you want—the success you desire.

ONLY THE FEW ARE EXTRAORDINARY

Even though the precepts are inconsistent, the nature and purposes of them are consistent, they are for success, and they are available for everyone to use. However, only the few will use them wisely and effectively and those few will achieve the pinnacles of managerial leadership. It is they who will truly become wise managers—powerful and successful manager/princes.

[H]ow much honor and fame, Cyrus gained by his humanity and affability, and by his not having exhibited a single instance of pride, cruelty, or luxuriousness, nor of any other of the vices that are apt to stain the lives of men.

(*The Discourses*: 378)

His [Camillus's] vigilance, prudence, magnanimity, and the good discipline and order which he observed in all his expeditions and in the command of his army, excited the admiration of his troops; [while] their hatred resulted from his being more severe in his punishments than generous in his rewards.

(*The Discourses*: 386)

[W]hat great services a good and wise man can render to his country, when his virtues and goodness have silenced envy, which so often prevents men from being useful by depriving them of the authority necessary for important occasions.

(*The Discourses*: 397)

BE WHAT YOU WANT TO BE

If you are presently a manager trying to achieve more, to reach new goals, you should be aware that the road to managerial success is difficult; it is bumpy and cluttered with risk. If you are afraid of risk, of challenges, then there is a safer course of action—a smooth road. You can decide that you do not have what it takes to be an excellent and wise manager, and you can choose to remain at your present level or even return to being a worker in an organization.

In fact, the life of a private citizen would be preferable to that of a king at the expense of the ruin of so many human beings. Nevertheless, whoever is unwilling to adopt the first and humane course must, if he wishes to maintain his power, follow the latter evil course. But men generally decide upon a middle course, which is most hazardous; for they know neither how to be entirely good or entirely bad.

(*The Discourses*: 156)

Or if you are not a manager yet but only thinking about becoming one, you may decide that it is best to remain a worker and not seek a management position.

Neither of these choices are inauspicious or imply that you lack common sense. It is not only wise managers but also wise individuals who recognize who they are and what they want to be. The thoughtful person is happy with the decisions he makes within and concerning organizations. People who believe that success in life is only determined by their status in an organization are exceedingly foolish.

And the manner in which we live, and that in which we ought to live, are things so wide asunder, that he who quits the one to betake himself to the other is more likely to destroy than to save himself.

(*The Prince*: 110)

THE CHALLENGE—GET OFF THE MIDDLE ROAD

So my challenge to you, indeed what should be your challenge to yourself, is to first decide what you want to be, then to chart your course in getting there. Go and do what you have set out to do. Never take the middle road. Become a thinker and a planner, a doer and achiever.

[H]alf measures should be avoided, these being most dangerous, as was proven by the Samnites, who, when they had hemmed the Romans in between the Caudine forks, disregarded the advice of an old man, who counselled them either to let the Romans depart honorably, or to kill them all. And by taking the middle course of disarming them and obliging them to pass under a yoke, they let them depart with shame and rage in their hearts. So that the Samnites soon after found, to their cost, how [wise] the old man's advice had been, and how injurious the course which they had adopted.

(*The Discourses*: 292)

Slow and [tardy] deliberations are not less injurious than indecision, . . . for tardiness helps no one, and generally injures yourself. It ordinarily arises from lack of courage or force, or from the evil disposition of those who have to deliberate, being influenced by passion to ruin the state or to serve some personal interests, and who therefore do not allow the deliberations to proceed, but thwart and impede them in every way.

(The Discourses: 262–63)

It is quite easy to plan for tomorrow and relatively easy to plan for the next year or the next five years, but it is more difficult to plan for the next ten to twenty years. But in today's fast-paced, high-tech, rapid-communication world, talk about the twenty-first century is common. The world is rapidly becoming a global village, and in any village or town it is important that the citizens have a purpose, a plan.

TOWARD THE YEAR 2525

To be a unique person, to reach for the stars, you must be capable of thinking forward to the year 2525 and beyond. This does not mean you should cultivate an unrealistic futuristic attitude; obviously there is not much chance that those reading this book in the 1990s will actually get there. But you must be confident that the ideas you have, or changes you promote, will have an effect on what the year 2525 is like and that it will be better because of you.

By projecting your thoughts to the future you are better able to gain not only a better perspective of the past, but an understanding of the present. You are better able to step out of, and into, the big picture at will, gaining a broad vision that will assist you in your journey toward success and power. In light of the future you can appreciate change and realize its importance, and you can be confident that everything you want and are prepared to work for is possible.

However, everyone cannot or will not be what they deserve to be. Most will read this book once, make some plans for the future, act toward reaching those plans for a few weeks or months, and then drift back toward the middle road. And this is to your advantage, because it means that there will be more occasions for you to be the one to truly achieve, to be not what you can become, but what you will become, if you act today and every day. Opportunity is knocking; will you answer? The moment has arrived; will you seize it?

Epilogue

I hope you have noticed when reading this book that I have used both the words love and Machiavellian when talking about management. Historically when people think of Machiavelli they do not think of love. And it is true that most of the time you will neither find nor will you compete with managers who understand either concept. Even less often will you find managers who understand the need and importance of using appropriate amounts of these ingredients. But most managers are ordinary, not extraordinary.

As a side note to the management of business organizations, I continue to think about power and the consequences it has, not only for business organizations but for political and governmental organizations, which are in fact business organizations, the only difference being the services they perform. The purpose of any nation is to serve its people first and others second, although, granted, the people of a nation are served by having a positive relationship with other nations.

The fact that nations conquer other nations is obvious. This can be both good and bad. But what is important to understand is that, at least in the short run, nations are more likely to be conquered through the economic might of other nations, through the productivity of their labor forces, than by the might of their military, although, from time to time, they will still use their generals and armed forces to enforce their economic decisions. And as I have indicated, victory in these battles depends upon which nation has managerial and business superiority.

It is probable that the goals of nations remain the same and that only their tactics change, that nations will continue to conquer nations, and that the victors will be those who are economically and managerially superior. One lesson that has been learned by the nations in the twentieth century is that wars result in no winners and that economic dominance has a whole lot of the advantages of military conquest. These are obviously lessons that could have been learned from the ancients.

When confronting opponents; the managers of McDonald's Hamburgers and General Motors, as well as managers everywhere in the United States and the USSR and indeed all around the world, should remember the words of Machiavelli:

[T]he [leader of an organization] should always mistrust any manifest error which he sees the enemy commit, as it invariably conceals some stratagem. For it is not reasonable to suppose that men will be so incautious. But the desire of victory often blinds men to that degree that they see nothing but what seems favorable to their object.

(The Discourses: 428–29)

Wise men say, and not without reason, that whoever wishes to foresee the future must consult the past; for human events ever resemble those of preceding times. This arises from the fact that they are produced by men who have been, and ever will be, animated by the same passions, and thus they must necessarily have the same results.

(The Discourses: 422)

Being cautious does not mean you are distrustful, but it does mean you are careful. Anticipating problems before they arise does not mean that you want them to happen, but that you want to solve them should they occur.

The reason these things are important for managers in the United States, England, Germany, Japan, Russia, and the rest of the world is that businesses are becoming the troops and armies of the twenty-first century. The managers and leaders of today's corporations are taking the role of the commanders and generals of old. The prevailing weapons of the twenty-first century will be those of economic sanctions and economic dominance. Therefore it becomes more important than ever that those who would lead their countries to fame and fortune, through both the public and private sectors, become wise managers within their respective organizations.

Every organization, regardless of its size, every worker in an organization, regardless of his position; and every industry, regardless of its product or service, is a part of a nation's strength. Therefore it is incumbent on us all to be the best at what we do. It is vital that every organization increase its productivity and its managerial and organizational competence.

And it is the obligation of all managers to seek wisdom and understanding as they lead their organizations into the twenty-first century.

FROM ME TO YOU

Many encounters with power and conflicts between opponents are never reported, yet they may have within them lessons that would be useful to others. Significant things happen daily that do not make the front pages of your local newspaper. Indeed, important things happen to you.

There may be an attempt to take over your organization or one you deal with, or there may be a clash of wills between you and another or between those you come into contact with. It may involve billions of dollars, or there may not be any monetary measurement. If it involves you, it is important. Write to me and let me know about your experiences. Perhaps you have a comment or a question that might be useful to others on your journey to becoming the best you can be. Do not keep your power conflicts secreted in your mind; that can be harmful. Often it helps just to talk about them. So if you don't know who to tell, share them with me. I am interested in your encounters with power, your wins and losses, your successes and failures. If you share your experiences with me, perhaps this sharing will act as a catharsis for your hurting or a catalyst for your achieving, and if you allow me to share them with others, then someone else may learn from your experiences.

Appendix 1
Management Maxims

The following are excerpts from selected discourses found in *The Prince, The Discourses on the First Ten Books of Titus Livy,* and *The Art of War.* I have categorized each with a key word, in order to assist you in thinking about management from a different perspective. However, within each maxim there are other ideas—other thoughts. The ideas, as they apply to you, will change with time—depending on your perspective and position when you are reading them.

While I have at times substituted management words (manager, organization, employees) for Machiavelli's words (prince, kingdom, state), most of the time I have utilized Machiavelli's own words. The prince then becomes the president or the chief executive officer, the manager or the supervisor, the leader or the executive. The state, republic, or kingdom become the department or the division, the group or the work-unit, the corporation or the multinational.

This enables you to "plug" yourself and your situation into each maxim. You might want to use the word "vice president" or "president" for "prince," and the words "manufacturing division" or "XYZ Company" for "the state," or you might want to use your own name or that of a subordinate or supervisor, and the name of your company or that of a competitor. Use what makes sense to you. This will help make each thought more meaningful to you and allow you to gain deeper insight into each one as your situation changes. And indeed that is what is important.

Note: The letters following each maxim indicate the following. *D* refers to *The Discourses*; *P* refers to *The Prince*; and *A* refers to *The Art of War*. The page number follows the letter. The full citation for each of these works is given in the bibliography.

You should keep notes with each maxim, expressing your feelings and ideas as you read. Be sure and place the date by each one. Then when you reread them, compare your prior thoughts with your current ones. Analyze how you have changed and how you should change. By doing this, you will gain an increased perspective on your management philosophy, and you will be able to set your management goals more effectively.

ABILITY

[I]t matters little whether a general adopts [a course of managing by love or fear], provided he be possessed of such high ability as to enable him to achieve success by either line of conduct; for . . . both have their defects and their dangers, unless compensated for by extraordinary talent and courage. (*D*: 380)

ACCIDENTS, PLANNING FOR

Sudden accidents are not easily prevented; but those which are foreseen are prevented without difficulty. (*A*: 520)

ACCIDENTS, TAKING ADVANTAGE OF

[When something happens that should not,] the Generals in times past when such an accident happened, immediately give some reason for it, and [blamed] it to some natural cause, or else [misstated the real reason it happened] and [changed] it to their own profit and advantage. (*A*: 507)

ACCOMPLICES

When the number of accomplices in a conspiracy exceeds three or four, it is almost impossible for it not to be discovered, either through treason, imprudence, or carelessness. The moment more than one of the conspirators is arrested, the whole plot is discovered; for it will be impossible for any two to agree perfectly as to all their statements. If only one be arrested, and he be a man of courage and firmness, he may be able to conceal the names of his accomplices; but then the others, to remain safe, must be equally firm, and not lay themselves open to discovery by flight, for if any one of them proves wanting in courage, whether it be the one that is arrested or one of those that are at liberty, the conspiracy is sure to be discovered. (*D*: 335)

ACCUSATIONS

[W]henever the aid of foreign powers is called in by any party in a [organization], it is to be ascribed to defects in its [structure], and more especially to the want of means for enabling the people to exhaust the malign humors that spring up among men, without having recourse to extraordinary measures; all of which can easily be provided against by instituting accusations before numerous judges, and giving these sufficient influence and importance. (*D*: 116)

ACCUSED

[M]any wise men [have said] that you may talk freely with one man about everything, for unless you have committed yourself in writing the "yes" of one man is worth as much as the "no" of another; and therefore one should guard most carefully against writing, as against a dangerous rock, for nothing will convict you quicker than your own handwriting. (*D*: 337)

ACQUISITION

A Prince cannot avoid giving offense to his new subjects, either in respect of the troops he quarters on them, or of some other of the numberless vexations attendant on a new acquisition. (*P*: 5)

When a newly acquired [organization] has been accustomed . . . to live under its own laws and in freedom, there are three methods whereby it may be held. The first is to destroy it; the second, to go and reside there in person; the third, to suffer it to live on under its own laws, subjecting it to a tribute, and entrusting its government to a few of the inhabitants who will keep it your friend. (*P*: 28)

[A]cquisitions sometimes prove most injurious even to a well-regulated republic, when they consist . . . in a city or province that has been enervated by pleasures and luxury; for these indulgences and habits become contagious by intercourse with the inhabitants. (*D*: 281)

ACTION

[In making a decision . . .] it [is of] the highest importance [to] think rather of what [you should do rather] than what [you should] say; when [you] have decided upon that, it will be easy to accommodate [your] words to [your] acts. (*D*: 262)

We must either go now at this very moment and carry [this plan] into execution, or I shall go and denounce you all, whereupon they all arose, and, without affording anyone time to repent, they carried their design into execution without difficulty. (*D*: 336)

ADAPTING

[Regardless of the manner of people's conduct] they are apt to exceed the proper limits, not being able always to observe the just middle course, they are apt to err in both. But he errs least and will be most favored by fortune who suits his proceedings to the times . . . and always follows the impulses of his nature. (*D*: 353)

ADVANTAGE

[I]f a general is unavoidably forced to engage in [a skirmish] against a new enemy, he should do so only with such advantages on his side as to expose him to no danger of defeat. (*D*: 415)

ADVANTAGE, BEING SURE YOU HAVE IT BEFORE BATTLE

[A] General is never to come to a field-fight unless he be constrained, or has some more than ordinary advantage. His advantage may [be] in the nature of the Place, in the discipline of his Army, or the number or excellence of his Men. (*A*: 483)

ADVANTAGE, USING IT

Nothing is of more importance in the whole art of War, than to know how to take advantage of what is offered. (*A*: 519)

ADVICE

History relates many instances of citizens having been sent into exile for having counselled enterprises that terminated unsuccessfully. (*D*: 410)

Certainly those who counsel princes and republics are placed between two dangers. If they do not advise what seems to them for the good of the [organization] or the prince, regardless of the consequences to themselves, then they fail of their duty and if they do advise it, then it is at the risk of their position and their lives; for all men are blind in this, that they judge of good or evil counsels only by the result. . . . [In order to avoid] this dilemma of either disgrace or danger, [there is] no other course than to take things moderately, and not to undertake to advocate any enterprise with too much zeal; but to give one's advice calmly and modestly. If then either the [organization] or the prince decides to follow it, they may do so, as it were, of their own will, and not as though they were drawn into it by your [persistence]. In adopting this course it is not reasonable to suppose that either prince or [organization] will manifest any ill will towards you on account of a resolution not taken contrary to the wishes of the many. For the danger arises when your advice has caused the many to be [contradicted]. In that case, when the result is unfortunate, they all concur in your destruction. And although by following [this course] you may fail to obtain that glory which is acquired by having been one against many in counselling an enterprise which success has justified, yet this is compensated for by two advantages. The first is, that you avoid all danger; and the second consists in the great credit which you will have if, after having modestly advised a certain course, your counsel is rejected, and the adoption of a different course results [in problems]. And although you cannot enjoy the glory acquired by the misfortunes of your [organization] or your prince, yet it must be held to be of some account. (*D*: 410)

ADVISORS

[C]onspiracies are generally made by the great, who have free access to the prince. (*D*: 333–34)

My business is to govern my subjects, to defend them, to prefer Peace; but yet to know how to manage myself in War; and if I have received honor or reward from the King, it is not for my understanding or experience in War, so much as for my integrity and counsel in times of Peace. A wise Prince ought not therefore to have any about him, but such as are constituted; for if they be too zealous either for Peace or for War, they will draw him into inconvenience. (*A*: 441)

There is nothing of more importance to the General of an Army, than to have about him persons that are faithful, experienced in war, and prudent in Counsel, with whom he may constantly advise, and confer about his own Men, and the Enemy . . . (*A*: 484)

AGREEMENTS

[I]t is never wise to enter into agreements the observance of which is doubtful. (*D*: 150)

ALLIANCES

And the usual course of things is that so soon as a formidable stranger enters a Province, all the weaker powers side with him, moved thereto by the ill-will they bear towards him who has hitherto ruled over them. (*P*: 11)

The reason why a confederation of [organizations] cannot well make extensive conquests is, that they are not a compact body, and do not have a central seat of power, which embarrasses consultation and concentrated action. It also makes them less desirous of dominion, for, being composed of numerous communities that are to share in this dominion, they do not value conquests as much as a single [organization] that expects to enjoy the exclusive benefit of them herself. (*D*: 239)

AMBITION

[A]nd what is still worse is that the haughty manners and insolence of the nobles and the rich excite in the breasts of those who have neither birth nor wealth, not only the desire to possess them, but also the wish to revenge themselves by depriving the former of those riches and honors which they see them employ so badly. (*D*: 109)

For as the nature of men is ambitious as well as suspicious, and puts no limits to one's good fortune, it is not impossible that the suspicion that may suddenly be aroused in the mind of the prince by the victory of the general may have been aggravated by some haughty expressions or insolent acts on his part; so that the prince will naturally be made to think of securing himself against the ambition of his general. And to do this, the means that suggest themselves to him are either to have the general killed, or to deprive him of that reputation which he has acquired with the prince's army and the people, by using every means to prove that the general's victory was not due to his skill and courage, but to chance and the cowardice of the enemy, or to the sagacity of the other captains who were with him in that action. (*D*: 159)

It was a saying of ancient writers, that men afflict themselves in evil, and become weary of the good, and that both these dispositions produce the same effects. For when men are no longer obliged to fight from necessity, they fight from ambition, which passion is so powerful in the hearts of men that it never leaves them, no matter to what height they may rise. (*D*: 174)

[F]or the ambition of the nobles is so great, that, if it is not repressed by various ways and means in any city, it will quickly bring that city to ruin. (*D*: 177)

[T]he Romans in the early beginning of their power already employed fraud, which it has ever been necessary for those to practice who from small beginnings wish to rise to the highest degree of power; and then it is the less censurable the more it is concealed. (*D*: 260)

[A]ny one whose ambition so far misleads him as to call in strangers to aid in his defense, or in an attack upon others, seeks to acquire that which he will not be able to hold, and which after acquiring will be easily taken from him. (*D*: 283–84)

[M]en always commit the error of not knowing where to limit their hopes, and by trusting to these rather than to a [honest] measure of their resources, they are generally ruined. (*D*: 305)

For men are so restless that the slightest opening for their ambition causes them quickly to forget all the affection [for those who have previously helped them]. (*D*: 379–80)

APPEARANCES

[I]f in other respects the old condition of things be continued, and there be no discordance in their customs, men live peaceably with one another. (*P*: 7)

[B]ecause men in general judge rather by the eye than by the hand, for all can see but few can touch. Everyone sees what you seem, but few know what you are, and these few dare not oppose themselves to the opinion of the many. (*P*: 129)

For the [average] are always taken by appearances and by results, and the world is made up of the [average], the few only finding room when the many have no longer ground to stand on. (*P*: 130)

APPREHENSION

[It is] dangerous . . . for [an organization] or a prince to keep the minds of their subjects in a state of apprehension by pains and penalties constantly suspended over their heads. (*D*: 191)

ARTIFICES

[A]rtifices may safely and with advantage be employed when they have more the appearance of reality than of fiction; for then their seeming strength will prevent the prompt discovery of their weakness. But when they are manifestly rather fictitious than real, they should either not be employed, or they should be kept at such a distance that their real character cannot be so quickly discovered. (*D*: 368).

ASSOCIATES

And to enable you to be thus powerful it becomes necessary to have associates, by whose aid you can increase the population of your own city . . . (*D*: 238)

ATTACK

[Follow the example of those who,] when assailed by a powerful enemy, their country being surrounded by mountains and rugged places, never attempted to combat the enemy in the passes or mountains, but have always gone either to meet him in advance of these, or, when they did not wish to do that, have awaited his coming in easy and open places. (*D*: 151)

For it was [the Romans'] custom [as] soon as war was declared to take the field immediately with their armies, and promptly to meet the enemy and give him battle; and when they had [won], the enemy (to save his country from being devastated) came to terms, and the Romans condemned him to cede a portion of his territory, which they converted into private possessions, or established colonies upon it, and which, from being situated upon their confines, served as a guard to the Roman frontier . . . (*D*: 243–44)

[T]here are but two motives for making war against a republic: one, the desire to subjugate her; the other, the apprehension of being subjugated by her. . . . If she remains quite within her limits, and experience shows that she entertains no ambitious projects, the fear of her power will never prompt any one to attack her; and this would even be more certainly the case if her constitution and laws prohibited all aggrandizement. (*D*: 113)

AUTHORITY

States governed by a sole Prince and his servants vest in him a more complete authority; because throughout the land none but he is recognized as sovereign, and if obedience be yielded to any others, it is yielded . . . to his ministers and officers for whom personally no special love is felt. (*D*: 23)

[T]he authority which is violently usurped, and not that which is conferred by the free suffrages of the people, is hurtful to republics. (*D*: 172)

["how useless it is] to confide the command of an army to several chiefs; for each one holding opinions of his own, which the others [would] not adopt, they afforded the enemy the opportunity to take advantage of their dissensions." [quoting Titus Livius (Livy)]. (D: 369)

AUXILIARY WORKERS

[A]uxiliary troops that are sent you by any prince are under officers appointed by him, under his banner, and are paid by him. . . . Such troops, when victorious, generally plunder as well him to whose assistance they were sent as the enemy against whom they have been employed; and this they do either from the [disloyalty] of the prince who sends them, or from their own ambition. (D: 283)

AVENGE

[There is danger following the execution of a plot] when someone is left who will avenge the prince that is killed. He may have [friends] or other relatives, who inherit the [organization], and who have been spared by your negligence . . . [who] will avenge the prince. (D: 344)

AVOID, THINGS TO

[T]he causes that most easily render a prince odious to his people, . . . is to deprive them of anything that is advantageous and useful to them; this they never forget, and the least occasion reminds them of it, and as these occur almost daily, their resentment is also daily revived. (D: 386)

[To] show yourself proud and presumptuous . . . is . . . most hateful to the people, . . . and although this pomp and pride may in no way inconvenience them, yet it renders those who indulge in it most odious. Princes, therefore, should carefully avoid this rock; for to incur hatred without any advantage is the greatest temerity and imprudence. (D: 386)

BARGAINING

[A]n authority conferred by the free suffrages of the people never harmed a republic, . . . presupposed that the people, in giving that power, would limit it, as well as the time during which it was to be exercised. But if from having been deceived, or from any other reason, they are induced to give this power imprudently . . . [then evil will come their way.] (D: 172)

BATTLE

It is well for a general not to risk the chance of battle with an enemy whose position is daily made worse by time and the disadvantages of the country. But in any other case a battle cannot be avoided without dishonor and danger. (D: 358)

[A] prince who has his people well armed and disciplined for war should always await a powerful and dangerous enemy at home, and should not go to meet him at a distance. But a prince whose subjects are unarmed, and the country unac-customed to war, should always keep it as far away from home as possible; and thus both one and the other will best defend themselves, each in his own way. (*D*: 258)

[R]eal courage, good discipline, and confidence founded upon so many victories cannot be extinguished by matters of such slight moment; nor can a vain idea inspire men animated by such feelings with fear, or a momentary disorder serious-ly injure them. (*D*: 405)

[A] well disciplined body of infantry can only be overcome with greatest difficul-ty, and then only by another body of infantry. (*D*: 276)

BATTLE, ONLY WHEN NECESSITY REQUIRES

A good General never comes to a Battle but when necessity requires, or some great advantage invites him. (*A*: 520)

BEING IN CHARGE

[W]hen arms have to be employed by a Prince, . . . the Prince ought to go in per-son to take command as captain. (*P*: 87)

BENEFITS

[T]o be [generous] with the property of others does not take from your reputa-tion, but adds to it. What injures you is to give away what is your own. (*P*: 117)

[Y]ou must bind men to you by benefits, or you must make sure of them in some other way, but never reduce them to the alternative of having either to destroy you or perish themselves. (*D*: 339)

CHANCES, TAKING WHEN NECESSARY

And his necessity consists in finding his condition such, that without fighting he must be certainly destroyed. . . . in [this] case a General is always to venture, though he fights [with the] disadvantage; for [it is] better fighting where fortune may favor you, than not to try her at all, and be certainly ruined; and in this case it would be as great a fault in . . . a General not to fight, as it would be if he had an opportunity of defeating his adversary, and was either too ignorant to know it, or too cowardly or [slow] to make use of it. (*A*: 483)

CHANGE

For Time, driving all things before it, may bring with it evil as well as good. (*P*: 14)

For no man is found prudent enough to adapt himself to . . . changes [from good times to bad times] because, having always prospered while pursuing one path, he cannot be persuaded that it would be well for him to leave it. And so when occasion requires the cautious man to act impetuously, he cannot do so and is undone; whereas, had he changed his nature with time and circumstances, his fortune would have been unchanged. (*P*: 187)

But as all human things are kept in a perpetual movement, and can never remain stable, [organizations] naturally either rise or decline, and necessity compels them to many acts to which reason will not influence them; so that, having organized a [company] competent to maintain herself without expanding, still, if forced by necessity to extend her territory, in such case we shall see her foundations give way and herself quickly brought to ruin. (*D*: 113)

[W]hen speaking of the danger of trying to abate an evil that has already attained a considerable growth . . . so that in the end the matter is reduced to [either endeavoring] to destroy the evil at the risk of sudden ruin, or, by allowing it to go on, submit to manifest servitude, unless the death of the individual or some other accident intervenes to rid the [organization] of him (*D*: 193)

That we cannot . . . change at will is due to two causes: the one is the impossibility of resisting the natural bent of our characters; and the other is the difficulty of persuading ourselves, after having been accustomed to success by a certain mode of proceeding, that any other can succeed as well. It is this that causes the varying success of a man; for the times change, but he does not change his mode of proceeding. (*D*: 355)

[There is the] love of novelty, which manifests itself equally in those who are well off and in those who are not. . . . [m]en get tired of prosperity, just as they are afflicted by the reverse. This love of change, then, so to speak, opens the way to everyone who takes the lead in any innovation in any country. If he is a stranger they run after him, and if he is of the country they surround him, increase his influence, and favor him in every way; so that, whatever his mode of proceeding and conduct may be, he will succeed in making rapid progress. (*D*: 379)

There is nothing that disturbs or impedes the actions of men more than when suddenly, and without time to reflect, the order of things agreed upon has to be entirely changed. And if such a change causes embarrassment in ordinary affairs, it does so to an infinitely greater degree in war or in conspiracies; for in such matters nothing is more essential than that men should firmly set their minds on performing the part that has been assigned to them. And if men have their minds fixed for some days upon a certain order and arrangement, and this is suddenly changed, it is impossible that this should not disturb them so as to defeat the whole plot. So that it is much better to carry out any such project according to the original plan, even if it should present some inconveniences, rather than to change the order agreed upon and incur a thousand embarrassments. And this will occur, if there be not time to reorganize the project entirely; for when there is time for that, men can suit themselves to the new order of things. (*D*: 340)

CHANGE, AGENTS OF

[W]hether innovators can stand alone, or whether they depend for aid upon others; in other words, whether to carry out their ends they must resort to [appeal], or can use force. In the former case they always fare badly and effect nothing; but when they depend upon themselves and can employ force, they seldom fail. (*P*: 35–36)

CHANGING TIMES

For any man accustomed to a certain mode of proceeding will never change it, . . . and consequently when time and circumstances change, so that his ways are no longer in harmony with them, he must of necessity succumb. (*D*: 354)

COMING TO TERMS

Princes or republics from a proper estimate of their forces will hardly ever be reduced to a condition similar to that of the Latins, who made terms with the Romans when they ought not to have done it, and declared war when they should not have done it; and so managed that both the friendship and the enmity of Rome proved equally injurious to them. (*D*: 289)

Princes that are attacked cannot then commit a greater error, especially when their assailant greatly exceeds them in power, than to refuse all accommodation, and more particularly when it has been offered; for no terms will ever be so hard but what they will afford some advantage to him who accepts them, so that he really obtains thereby a share of the victory. (*D*: 304)

[I]f any one desires a people or a prince to abandon all ideas of a peaceful settlement with another, then there is no more certain and effectual way than to make them commit some outrageous act against those with whom you wish to prevent them from making peace. For the fear of punishment which they are conscious of having deserved by that outrage will ever keep them from coming to terms. (*D*: 403).

[W]hen the [battle] is lost, a wise General is to consider the best that he can make of it, especially if there be any thing of his Army remaining. (*A*: 482)

COMMUNICATIONS

[A] good commander should, . . . [among] his other regulations, specially appoint persons to receive his orders and transmit them to the others; and he should accustom his soldiers not to listen to any but their regular officers, and direct the officers to give no orders but such as emanate from the commander. The nonobservance of this rule has often caused the greatest misfortunes. (*D*: 367)

[M]any Armies have been ruined when the Captain's orders have been mistaken, or not heard; for which reason the words of Command in such great dangers ought to be clear and intelligible. . . . If your commands are by word of mouth you must use particular, and be sure to avoid general terms, and in your particular words you must be cautious to use none that may be liable to an ill interpretation. (*A*: 491)

COMPETITORS

[Among] the other indications by which the power of [an organization] may be recognized is the relation in which they live with their neighbors; if these are tributary to her by way of securing her friendship and protection, then it is a sure sign that that [organization] is powerful. But if these neighboring [organizations], though they may be more feeble than herself, draw money from her, then it is a sure indication of great weakness on the part of the [organization]. (*D*: 310)

COMPLAINTS

[H]ow useful and necessary it is for a republic to have laws that afford to the masses the opportunity of giving vent to the hatred they may have conceived against any citizen; for if there exist no legal means for this, they will resort to illegal ones, which beyond doubt produce much worse effects. (*D*: 115)

CONFIDENCE

[O]nce having lost the pass which you had hoped to hold, and upon which your people and army had confidently relied, they are generally seized with such terror that they are lost, without your having ever been able to test their courage; and thus you lose your whole fortune from having risked only a portion of your forces. (*D*: 152)

To insure victory the troops must have confidence in themselves as well as in their commander. (*D*: 404)

Never bring your men to fight till you have some just confidence in their courage, till you have seen them well armed, and well ordered; and never let them engage but when you find them cheerily, and hopeful of success. (*A*: 519)

CONFLICTS

[D]ivisions purposely caused can [never] lead to good; on the contrary, when an enemy approaches, divided [organizations] are lost at once, because the weaker faction will always side with the invader, and the other will be unable to stand alone. (*P*: 156)

CONFORMING TO THE TIMES

[M]en in their conduct, and especially in their most prominent actions, should well consider and conform to the times in which they live. And those who, from an evil choice or from natural inclination, do not conform to the times in which they live, will in the most instances live unhappily, and their undertakings will come to a bad end; [while], on the contrary, success attends those who conform to the times. (*D*: 352)

CONGLOMERATES

And the hardest of all servitudes is to be subject to a [conglomerate], and this for these reasons: first, because it is more enduring, and there is no hope of escaping from it; and secondly, because [conglomerates] aim to enervate and weaken all other [organizations] so as to increase their own power. (*D*: 234)

CONSPIRACIES

But even if [a] conspiracy is not discovered in its progress, yet a thousand difficulties will arise in its execution; for if you arrive a little before or a little after the appointed moment, all is [spoiled]. The least unusual noise, . . . the slightest change in the order agreed upon, or the least fault or smallest error, will involve the whole enterprise in ruin. To these difficulties add the darkness of night, which naturally increases the apprehensions of those engaged in such hazardous enterprises; and as the greater part of the men employed in such expeditions are wholly unacquainted with the situation of the country or the place where they are led, the slightest unforeseen accident confounds them and fills them with fear and trouble, so that the merest shadow will cause them to turn back. (*D*: 316)

Conspiracies against single individuals are generally apt to fail, . . . but when undertaken against two or more persons, they fail much easier. . . . In fact, to strike two blows of this kind at the same instant and in different places is impracticable, and to attempt to do so at different moments of time would certainly result in the one's preventing the other. So that, if it is imprudent, rash, and doubtful to conspire against a single prince, it amounts to folly to do so against two at the same time. (*D*: 342)

[W]hen conspiracies are feeble, they can and ought to be crushed as promptly as possible. (*D*: 349)

CONSPIRACIES, AGAINST ORGANIZATIONS

Conspiracies against the [organization] are less dangerous for those engaged in them than plots against the life of the sovereign. In their conduct there is not so much danger, in their execution there is the same, and after execution there is none. In the conduct of the plot the danger is very slight, for a citizen may aspire to supreme power without manifesting his intentions to any one; and if nothing interferes with his plans, he may carry them through successfully, or if they are thwarted by some law, he may await a more favorable moment, and attempt it by another way. (*D*: 345)

CONSPIRACIES, DISCOVERY OF

[The discovery of conspiracies] is either by denunciation or by surmises. Denunciation is the consequence of treachery or of want of prudence on the part of those to whom you confide your designs; and treachery is so common that you cannot safely impart your project to any but such of your most trusted friends as are willing to risk their lives for your sake, or to such other malcontents as are equally desirous of the prince's ruin. Of such reliable friends you may find one or two; but as you are necessarily obliged to extend your confidence, it becomes impossible to find many such, for their devotion to you must be greater than their sense of danger and fear of punishment. (*D*: 334)

If [princes or organizations] discover that a conspiracy exists against them, they must, before punishing its authors, endeavor carefully to know its nature and extent—to weigh and measure well the means of the conspirators, and their own strength. And if they find it powerful and alarming, they must not expose it until they have provided themselves with sufficient force to crush it, as otherwise they will only hasten their own destruction. They should therefore try to simulate ignorance of it, for if the conspirators should find themselves discovered, they will be forced by necessity to act without consideration. (*D*: 348)

Discovery from lack of prudence occurs when any one of the conspirators speaks incautiously, so that [someone] overhears it. . . . Or it may occur from thoughtlessness, when someone communicates the secret to his wife or child, or to some other indiscreet person. (*D*: 335)

A prince or a republic who, for their own advantage, wish to defer the disclosure of a conspiracy, cannot use a more effectual means for that purpose than artfully to hold out to the conspirators the prospect of an early and favorable opportunity for action; so that, [while] waiting for that, or persuaded that they have ample time, the prince or [organization] will themselves gain time to overwhelm the conspirators. Those who act differently will accelerate their own ruin. (*D*: 348)

CONTROL

[T]he character of the people is not to be blamed any more than that of princes, for both alike are liable to err when they are without any control. (*D*: 216)

For a prince who knows no other control but his own will is like a madman, and a people that can do as it pleases will hardly be wise. (*D*: 218)

CONVICTED

You may escape, then, from the accusation of a single individual, unless you are convicted by some writing or other pledge, which you should be careful never to give. (*D*: 338)

COURAGE

For it is impossible that one should not be confused at such a moment [of carrying out a dangerous act], even though possessed of firmness and courage, and accustomed to the use of the sword and to seeing men killed. Therefore only men experienced in such affairs should be chosen as the instruments of execution, and none other should be trusted, though they be reputed to be most courageous; for you cannot be sure of any man's courage in great affairs, unless it has been tested by actual experience. For the confusion of the mind at the important moment may cause the sword to drop from a man's hand, or may make him say things that will be equally ruinous. (*D*: 342)

[W]hen a number of princes combine to make war upon a single one, the latter will triumph over the combination, provided he has courage and strength enough to resist the first shock and bide events by temporizing. But if he cannot do this, he is exposed to a thousand dangers. (*D*: 360)

DECEIT

Although deceit is detestable in all other things, yet in the conduct of war it is laudable and honorable; and a commander who vanquishes an enemy by stratagem is equally praised with one who gains victory by force. . . . I do not confound such deceit with [infidelity], which breaks pledged faith and treaties; for although [organizations and empires] may at times be won by [infidelity], yet will it ever bring dishonor with it. But I speak of those [gambits] and stratagems which you employ against an enemy that distrusts you, and in the employment of which properly consists the art of war. (*D*: 419–20)

DECISION MAKING

Before deciding upon any course, . . . men should well consider the objections and dangers which it presents; and if its perils exceed its advantages, they should avoid it, even though it had been in accordance with their previous determination; for to do otherwise would expose them to [great danger]. (*D*: 203)

DEFENSE

[T]here is not a more ineffectual and hazardous mode of defending a [organization] than to do it in a disorderly and tumultuous manner. (*D*: 399)

[A] want of proper judgment sometimes causes men, who are incompetent to defend themselves, to engage in war for the defense of others. (*D*: 254)

DELEGATION

[A]lthough one man alone should organize a government, yet it will not endure long if the administration of it remains on the shoulders of a single individual;

it is well, then, to confide this to the charge of many, for thus it will be sustained by the many. (*D*: 121)

DELIBERATIONS

[I]t will always happen that in doubtful cases, where prompt resolution is required, there will be this indecision when weak men have to deliberate and resolve. (*D*: 262)

DESIRES

[N]ature has created men so that they desire everything, but are unable to attain it; desire being thus always greater than the faculty of acquiring, discontent with what they have and dissatisfaction with themselves result from it. This causes the changes in their fortunes. (*D*: 174)

DISCIPLINE

[M]en are less careful how they offend him who makes himself loved than him who makes himself feared. For love is held by the tie of obligation, which, because men are a sorry breed, is broken on every prompting of self-interest; but fear is bound by the apprehension of punishment which never loosens its grasp. (*P*: 120–21)

[I]t ought to be perceived that where good discipline prevails there also will good order prevail, and good fortune rarely fails to follow. (*D*: 105)

For the wounds and every other evil that men inflict upon themselves spontaneously, and of their own choice, are in the long run less painful than those inflicted by others. (*D*: 171)

[D]iscipline in an army [is necessary], not only to make them combat with order, but also to prevent any slight accident from creating confusion. (*D*: 366–67)

DISSENSIONS

[D]issensions in [organizations] are generally the result of idleness and peace, [while] apprehension and war are productive of union. (*D*: 300)

DISTURBANCES

[W]hoever is at the head of an army, or whoever happens to be a [leader in an organization] where sedition has broken out, should present himself before the multitude with all possible grace and dignity, and attired with all the insignia of his rank, so as to inspire the more respect. (*D*: 207)

DOUBT

[F]or it is impossible to explain one's self properly when in doubt and indecision as to what is to be done; but once resolved and decided, it is easy to find suitable words. (*D*: 262)

DO UNTO OTHERS

[N]ecessity may force you to do unto the prince that which you see the prince about to do to you; the danger of which may be so pressing as not to afford you the time to provide for your own safety. Such a necessity ordinarily insures success. (*D*: 338)

EDUCATION

Nor is there any better or more convenient means of acquiring a knowledge of countries than the chase [practice and experience with many types of organizations]; for it makes those who indulge in it perfectly familiar with the character of the country. And it is a fact that a man who has familiarized himself thoroughly with one [organization] afterwards readily comprehends the nature of all other [organizations]; for all [organizations] resemble each other in their general conformation, so that the knowledge of one facilitates the knowledge of others. But a man who has never acquired a practical knowledge of one, rarely or perhaps never attains the knowledge of another . . . unless after a great length of time. But he who has that practice will at a glance know how such a plain lies, how such a mountain rises, or where such a valley leads; and all similar things which his former practice has taught him. (*D*: 418)

EMPIRE

If therefore you wish to make a people numerous and warlike, so as to create a great empire, you will have to constitute it in such manner as will cause you more difficulty in managing it; and if you keep it either small or unarmed, and you acquire other dominions, you will not be able to hold them, or you will become so feeble that you will fall a prey to whoever attacks you. (*D*: 112)

EMPLOYEE GOODWILL

[A]nd therefore [organizations] as well as princes should think in advance what adversities may befall them, and of whom they may have need in time of trouble, and then they should [harmonize] themselves towards these in the manner they might deem necessary in case danger would come upon them. And whoever acts differently, . . . and supposes . . . that it is time enough by benefits to secure the good will of the people when danger has come upon him, deceives himself greatly; for not only will he fail to obtain the good will of the people, but he will accelerate his own destruction. (*D*: 166)

[H]e best secures himself [against secret plots] when he escapes being hated or despised, and keeps on good terms with his people. (*P*: 133)

EMPLOYEE RIGHTS

[F]or it is not well that [an organization] should be constituted in such fashion that a citizen can be oppressed without recourse for having promulgated a law for the benefit of liberty. (D: 198)

EMPLOYEES

[A] city accustomed to live in freedom, if it is to be preserved at all, is more easily controlled through its own citizens than in any other way. (P: 28–29)

He who becomes a Prince through the favor of the people should keep on good terms with them; which it is easy for him to do, since all they ask is not to be oppressed. (P: 69)

[A]nd he will find that a small part of them wish to be free for the purpose of commanding, [while] all the others, who constitute an immense majority, desire liberty so as to be able to live in greater security. (D: 139–40)

But the infantry must ever be regarded and valued as the very foundation and nerve of an army. (D: 275)

ENEMIES

[E]nemies who remaining, although vanquished, in their own homes, have power to hurt. (P: 10)

[H]e who has but a few enemies can easily make sure of them without great scandal, but he who has the masses hostile to him can never make sure of them, and the more cruelty he employs the feebler will his authority become; so that his best remedy is to try and secure the good will of the people. (D: 139)

ENEMIES, DIVIDING THE FORCES OF

A General above all things is to endeavor to divide the Enemies' Forces, either by rendering his Confidants suspicious; or by giving him occasion to separate his Troops, and by consequence weaken himself. (A: 506)

ENEMIES, KNOWING THEIR SECRETS

If you design to understand the secrets of your Enemy, and to know his order and condition; you must do as others have done, send Ambassadors to him, with wise and experienced Soldiers, . . . who may take their opportunity to view his Army, and consider his strength and weakness so [you can find an] occasion to overcome him. Some have pretended to banish some one of their Confidants, and by that means had information of his Enemies' designs. (A: 505)

ENEMIES, NOT BOXING IN

[G]reat care is to be [taken] never to bring your Enemy to despair. Caesar was very cautious of this in his War with the Germans, and opened a way for them, when he saw that not being able to fly, they must of necessity fight, and that more courageously than otherwise; wherefore he chose rather the trouble of pursuing them when they fled, than the danger of fighting them when they were forced to defend themselves. (*A*: 508)

ENEMIES, NOT UNDERESTIMATING

[N]ever fancy your enemy so weak as not to understand his own business: on the contrary . . . you would be less exposed to his stratagems, and run [less] danger, the weaker and more careless you observe him to be, the more you are to [understand] him. In this case you are to [act] in two different manners, you are to fear him in your own thoughts, and order your affairs accordingly; but in your words and outward behavior you are to seem to despise him; and this last way makes your Soldiers more confident of Victory, the other makes you more cautious, and less apt to be [taken advantage of]. (*A*: 493)

ENTHUSIASM

[H]e who attacks acts with more spirit than he who awaits the attack, and so inspires the troops with greater confidence; by attacking the enemy in his own country, you deprive him also of many advantages in availing of his resources; his subjects, who are plundered, can afford him no assistance, and the presence of the enemy constrains the prince to be more considerate in exacting money or too many other services from them. . . . Besides, the attacking troops, being in a strange country, feel the necessity of fighting, which very necessity inspires them with greater courage. (*D*: 257)

EXAMPLE

Let not princes complain of the faults committed by the people subjected to their authority, for they result entirely from their own negligence or bad example. . . . The example of the prince is followed by the masses, who keep their eyes always turned upon their chief. (*D*: 395–96)

[A leader must before battle have] filled his soldiers with the same spirit that animates himself, and if he has not trained them promptly and precisely to obey his orders, he will inevitably be beaten. (*D*: 402)

EXECUTION OF PLOTS

The first and most certain [way to avoid being discovered in the carrying out of a plot, in fact the only one], is not to afford your associates in the plot any time to betray you; and therefore you should confide your project to them at the moment of its execution, and not sooner. Those who act thus are most likely to escape [the dangers to be found in plotting] and therefore have their enterprises almost always succeeded. (*D*: 336)

EXPLAINING

[T]he quickest way of opening the eyes of the people is to find the means of making them descend to particulars, seeing that to look at things only in a general way deceives them. (*D*: 196).

EXTRAORDINARY ACTIONS

[I]n a well-ordered republic it should never be necessary to resort to extra-constitutional measures; for although they may for the time be beneficial, yet the precedent is pernicious, for if the practice is once established of disregarding the laws for good objects, they will in a little while be disregarded under the pretext for evil purposes. (*D*: 170-71)

FEAR

Fear and suspicion are so natural to princes that they cannot defend themselves against them, and thus it is impossible for them to show gratitude to those who, by victories achieved under their banners, have made important conquests for them. (*D*: 160)

FORCED AGREEMENTS

[A]greements which are the result of force will no more be observed by a prince than by [an organization], and where either the one or the other is apprehensive of losing . . . their [organization], to save it both will break their [word] and be guilty of ingratitude. (*D*: 219)

FORECASTING

[B]oth ancient and modern instances prove that no great events ever occur in any city or country that have not been predicted by soothsayers, revelations, or by portents and other celestial signs. (*D*: 212)

Wise men say, and not without reason, that whoever wishes to foresee the future must consult the past; for human events ever resemble those of preceding times. This arises from the fact that they are produced by men who have been, and ever will be, animated by the same passions, and thus they must necessarily have the same results. (*D*: 422)

FRAUD

[T]here was [never] a man who from obscure condition arrived at great power by merely employing open force; but there are many who have succeeded by fraud alone. (*D*: 259)

FRIENDS

[I]t is far easier to secure the friendship of those who being satisfied with things as they stood, were for that very reason his enemies, than of those who sided with him and aided him in his usurpation only because they were discontented. (P: 159)

GENERAL GOOD, THE

[F]or it is not individual prosperity, but the general good, that makes cities great; and certainly the general good is regarded nowhere but in [open organizations], because whatever they do is for the common benefit, and should it happen to prove an injury to one or more individuals, those for whose benefit the thing is done are so numerous that they can always carry the measure against the few that are injured by it. (D: 280–81)

GLORY

[E]ven in losing a battle a commander should at least endeavor to save his glory; and surely there is more glory in being overcome by force than in losing from any other cause. (D: 358)

GOOD OLD DAYS

When, however, adversity comes, [after things are thought to be good and] the error is discovered . . . then the people fly for safety to those whom in prosperity they had neglected. (D: 286)

GOODWILL

For however strong your armaments may be, it is essential that in entering a new Province you should have the goodwill of its inhabitants. (P: 5)

GREED

[A]s the vice of ingratitude is usually the consequence of either [greed] or fear, it will be seen that the peoples never fall into this error from [greed], and that fear also makes them less liable to it than princes, inasmuch as they have less reason for fear. (D: 161)

GRIEVANCES

Nothing, on the other hand, renders [an organization] more firm and stable, than to [structure] it in such a way that the excitement of the [bad dispositions] that agitate [an organization] may have a way prescribed by law for venting itself. (D: 114)

GROUPS

[A]s Princes cannot escape being hated by some, they should, in the first place, endeavor not to be hated by a class; failing wherein, they must do all they can to escape the hatred of the class which is the stronger. (*P*: 140)

[N]othing can better illustrate the character of a multitude than this example; for they are often audacious and loud in their denunciations of the decisions of their rulers, but when punishment stares them in the face, then, distrustful of each other, they rush to obey. Thus we see that whatever may be said of the good or evil disposition of the people is of little consequence, if you are well prepared to assert and maintain your authority should they be well disposed, and to defend yourself if their disposition be otherwise. (*D*: 213–14)

GUARD, KEEPING YOURS UP

Those who are in any fear of being [taken over], are to keep diligent guard as well when the Enemy is at a distance, as at hand; and they are to have most care of those places where they think themselves most secure; for many Towns have been lost by being assaulted on that side where they thought themselves impregnable. (*A*: 516)

GUILTY CONSCIENCE

[F]alse apprehensions are not to be disregarded and should be carefully considered, the more so as it is very easy to be surprised by them; for a man who has a guilty conscience readily thinks that everybody is speaking of him. You may overhear a word spoken to someone else that will greatly disturb you, because you think it has reference to you, and may cause you either to discover the conspiracy by flight, or embarrass its execution by hastening it before the appointed time. And this will happen the more easily the more accomplices there are in the conspiracy. (*D*: 343–44)

HALFWAY MEASURES

[You should] not take any halfway measures, [which] are always [deadly], and never make a friend nor rid yourself of an enemy. (*D*: 420)

HATRED

For when a prince has drawn upon himself universal hatred, it is reasonable to suppose that there are some particular individuals whom he has injured more than others, and who therefore desire to revenge themselves. This desire is increased by seeing the prince held in general aversion. A prince, then, should avoid incurring such universal hatred. (*D*: 330)

HONOR

Honor consists in being able, and knowing when and how, to chastise evildoers; and a prince who fails to punish them, so that they shall not be able to do any more harm, will be regarded as either ignorant or cowardly. (*D*: 291)

HUMANITY

[A]n act of humanity and benevolence will at all times have more influence over the minds of men than violence and ferocity. (*D*: 377)

INDECISION

[I]t is well in all deliberations to come at once to the essential point, and not always to remain in a state of indecision and uncertainty. (*D*: 262)

INFLUENCE

[Organizations] should make it one of their aims to watch that none of their [employees] should be allowed to do harm on pretense of doing good, and that no one should acquire an influence that would injure instead of promoting liberty. (*D*: 193)

INFLUENCE, GAINING

[A]ttention must be given to the means employed by citizens for acquiring such influence, and these are twofold, either public or private. The former are when a citizen gains reputation and influence by serving the [organization] well with his counsels or his actions. . . . But when they are acquired by private means, then they become most dangerous and [deadly]. Those private ways consist in benefiting this or the other private individual, by lending them money, marrying their daughters, sustaining them against the authority of the magistrates, and bestowing upon them such other favors as to make partisans of them. This encourages those who are thus favored to corrupt the public and to outrage the laws. A [well-managed organization], therefore, should open the way to public honors to those who seek reputation by means that are conducive to the public good; and close it to those whose aim is the advancement of private ends. (*D*: 394–95)

INGRATITUDE

[T]he vice of ingratitude springs either from [greed] or fear. (*D*: 159)

INJURIES

[P]rinces . . . will never be safe so long as those live whom they have deprived of their possessions; and [every prince should know] that old injuries can never be cancelled by new benefits, and the less so when the benefits are small in proportion to the injury inflicted. (*D*: 327)

INSOLENCE

[F]or insolence in prosperity and abjectness in adversity are the result of habit and education. If this be vain and feeble, then their conduct will likewise be without energy. (*D*: 401)

INSTRUCTIONS, NEED FOR OTHERS TO FOLLOW

[I]t is not enough to contrive good orders, unless they be strictly observed. (*A*: 501)

INTENTIONS

[F]or the enemy it is easy to come in full force, for his intention is to pass, and not to stop there; [while] on the contrary he who has to await the approach of the enemy cannot possibly keep so large a force there, for the reason that he will have to establish himself for a longer time in those confined and sterile places, not knowing when the enemy may come to make the attempt to pass. (*D*: 152)

INTENTIONS, KEEP FROM ENEMY

You must endeavor that your Enemy may not know how you intend to draw up your Army when you come to fight. (*A*: 520)

IRRESOLUTION

[I]rresolute [organizations] never take a wise course except by force; for their weakness never allows them to resolve upon anything where there is a doubt; and if that doubt is not overcome by some force they remain forever in a state of suspense. (*D*: 180)

JEALOUSY

It ever has been, and ever will be the case, that men of rare and extraordinary merit are neglected by [organizations] in times of peace and tranquility; for jealous of the reputation which such men have acquired by their virtues, there are always in such times many other citizens, who want to be, not only their equals, but their superiors. (*D*: 370)

KNOWLEDGE

[T]wo armies opposed to each other may both be equally damaged, and suffering from the same [cause]; in such case, the victory will be for him who is first informed of the condition of the other. (*D*: 375)

[M]en are apt to deceive themselves upon general matters, but not so much so when they come to particulars. (*D*: 194)

LEADERSHIP

[W]here the mass of the people is sound, disturbances and tumults do no serious harm; but where corruption has penetrated the people, the best laws are of no avail, unless they are administered by a man of such supreme power that he may cause the laws to be observed until the mass has been restored to a healthy condition. (*D*: 142)

A prince, to avoid the necessity of living in constant mistrust or of being ungrateful, should command all his expeditions in person. . . . For if victorious, all the glory and fruits of their conquests will be theirs; but if they are not present themselves at the action, and the glory of victory falls to the share of another, then it will seem to them that the conquest will not profit them unless they extinguish that glory of another which they have failed to achieve themselves. Thus they become ungrateful and unjust, and in that way their loss will be greater than their gain. (*D*: 162)

[Commanders] often opened the way for the enemy to retreat, which they might easily have barred; and closed it to their own soldiers for whom they could with ease have kept it open. Whoever then desires that a city should make an obstinate resistance, or that an army should fight with determination in the field, should above all things endeavor to inspire them with the conviction of the necessity for their utmost efforts. (*D*: 361)

[N]othing is so apt to restrain an excited multitude as the reverence inspired by some grave and dignified man of authority who opposes them. (*D*: 207)

[I]f either one of the two, the army or the commander, be good, they will be apt to make the other good likewise. But a good army without an able commander often becomes insolent and dangerous, . . . [y]ou can more safely rely upon a competent general, who has the time to instruct his men and the facilities for arming them, than upon an insolent army with a chief [wildly] chosen by them. (*D*: 365).

Those generals, therefore, deserve double praise and glory who not only had to conquer, but had actually to form and train their troops before meeting the enemy. For in this they have shown that twofold merit the union of which is so rare that many commanders, if they had been obliged to perform the same task, would not have obtained that celebrity which they have achieved. (*D*: 365)

[I]t is better to confide any expedition to a single man of ordinary ability, rather than to two, even though they are men of the highest merit, and both having equal authority. (*D*: 369–70)

[F]or the purpose of showing how a great man conduct himself, [the statement has been quoted] "My courage has neither been inflated by the dictatorship nor abated by exile." These words show that a truly great man is ever the same under all circumstances; and if his fortune varies, exalting him at one moment and oppressing him at another, he himself never varies, but always preserves a firm courage, which is so closely interwoven with his character that everyone can readily see that the fickleness of fortune has no power over him. The conduct of weak men is very different. Made vain and intoxicated by good fortune, they attribute their success to merits which they do not possess, and this makes them odious and insupportable to all around them. And when they have afterwards to meet a reverse of fortune, they quickly fall into the other extreme, and become abject and vile. Thence it comes that princes of this character think more of flying in adversity than of defending themselves, like men who, having made a bad use of prosperity, are wholly unprepared for any defense against reverses. (*D*: 399–400)

[A] commander cannot depend upon untrained soldiers who have learned nothing, nor can he expect them to do anything well. (*D*: 402)

Wishing to inspire them with confidence, which he felt to be the more necessary as they were in a country entirely new to them and opposed to an enemy whom they had not met before, he addressed his troops before going into battle; and after giving them many reasons for anticipating victory, he said "that he could give them other good reasons that would make their victory certain, but that it would be dangerous to reveal them at that moment." This artifice so judiciously employed well deserves to be imitated. (*D*: 405)

[A] good captain should avoid every unimportant action that may nevertheless produce a bad effect upon his army. For he must be altogether reckless to engage in any action in which he cannot employ his entire force, and where yet he hazards his whole fortune. . . . [o]n the other hand, . . . a prudent general, who has to encounter a new and untried enemy that has a reputation, should, before engaging in a general action, afford his troops the opportunity of testing such an enemy by slight skirmishes; so that, by learning to know him somewhat, and how to meet him, they may be relieved of any fear which the fame and report of the enemy may have caused them. I look upon this as a most essential duty of a general; in fact, he will feel the necessity of it himself when he sees that he would be marching to certain defeat, unless by some such slight experience he first removes the terror which the enemy's reputation may have engendered in the hearts of his troops. (*D*: 414)

LEADERSHIP, NEED TO HAVE COMMUNICATIONS SKILLS FOR

It is an easier matter to persuade or [discourage] anything with a small number of persons, because if words will not do, you have force of authority to back them; but the difficulty is to remove an opinion out of the heads of the multitude when it is contrary to your own judgment, or to the interest of the public; for there you can use nothing but words, which must be heard and understood by everybody, if you would have everybody convinced. For this reason it is requisite that an excellent General should be a good Orator, to inflame or assuage the courage of his Soldiers as he has occasion. (*A*: 485)

LEARNING, NEED FOR SELF-TEACHING

[The knowledge of The Art of War is] not sufficient, unless [you have the] ability to [learn on your] own; for never [was] any man . . . Master of a Trade, who had no [ideas] of his own; and if [ideas] be honorable in anything, it is most certainly in this. (*A*: 521)

LOSING WHAT YOU SHOULDN'T

[T]he loss of any place that a general abandons, without his army having experienced any reverse, will neither dim the glory of his arms nor his hope of victory. But the loss becomes a danger and real misfortune when you had intended to defend it, and everyone believes that you attempted to do so; it is then that a matter of so little moment may cause the loss of the whole war. (*D*: 415)

LOYALTY

[B]y [taking resources away from employees], you at once give offense, since you show your subjects that you distrust them, either as doubting their courage, or as doubting their fidelity, each of which [causes] hatred against you. (*P*: 154)

A[n organization] can and should have more hope and confidence in that [employee] who from a superior grade descends to accept a less important one, than in him who from an inferior employment mounts to the exercise of a superior one; for the latter cannot reasonably be relied upon unless he is surrounded by men of such respectability and virtue that his inexperience may in some measure be compensated for by their counsel and authority. (*D*: 174)

Moreover, men are very apt to deceive themselves as to the degree of attachment and devotion which others have for them, and there are no means of ascertaining this except by actual experience, but experience in such matters is of the utmost danger. And even if you should have tested the fidelity of your friends on other occasions of danger, yet you cannot conclude from that that they will be equally true to you on an occasion that presents infinitely greater dangers than any other. If you attempt to measure a man's good faith by the discontent which he manifests towards the prince, you will be easily deceived, for by the very fact of communicating to him your designs, you give him the means of putting an end to his discontent; and to insure his fidelity, his hatred of the prince or your influence over him must be very great. (*D*: 334)

But of all the perils that follow the execution of a conspiracy, none is more certain and none more to be feared than the attachment of the people to the prince that has been killed. There is no remedy against this, for the conspirators can never secure themselves against a whole people. (*D*: 345)

LOYALTY, SUSPECTING

If you suspect the [loyalty of others] and would assure yourself of them, and surprise them [without warning], you cannot do better than to communicate some design with them, desire their assistance, and pretend to some farther enterprize, without the least [resentment] or suspicion of them: and by doing so, (not imagining you have any jealousy of him) he will neglect his own defense, and give you opportunity of effecting your designs. (*A*: 505)

MALCONTENTS

[H]e who conspires always reckons on pleasing the people by putting the Prince to death; but when he sees that instead of pleasing he will offend them , he cannot summon courage to carry out his design. (*P*: 133–34)

And as to [the] vain hopes and promises [of exiles], such is their extreme desire to return to their homes that they naturally believe many things that are not true, and add many others on purpose; so that, with what they really believe and what they say they believe, they will fill you with hopes to that degree that if you attempt to act upon them you will incur a fruitless expense, or engage in an undertaking that will involve you in ruin. (*D*: 313)

MALCONTENTS, USE OF

When any come over to your service from the Enemy, they are of great advantage to you, provided they be faithful; for it is more diminution to the Enemies' strength to have Soldiers revolt, than to have so many slain, though the name of a fugitive is suspicious to new friends, and abominable to old. (*A*: 519)

MANAGEMENT BY DECEPTION

[A] prince who wishes to achieve great things must learn to deceive. (*D*: 259)

MANAGEMENT BY FEAR

Wherever fear dominates, there we shall find [lack of trust] in [both an organization and a manager] although the same influence may cause either a [manager] or [an organization] to keep [its word] at the risk of ruin. (*D*: 220)

[M]en are prompted in their actions by two main motives, namely, love and fear; so that he who makes himself beloved will have as much influence as he who makes himself feared, although generally he who makes himself feared will be more readily followed and obeyed than he who makes himself beloved. (*D*: 379)

MANAGEMENT BY FORCE

[I]t was said by a wise man, that to hold the government of [an organization] by violence, it was necessary that there should be a proper proportion between him who holds by force and those whom he thus subjects to his control. And whenever that just proportion exist, he may expect his tenure of power to be enduring. But when the oppressed is more powerful than the oppressor, then the latter will daily have occasion to fear his overthrow. (*D*: 382)

MANAGEMENT, GOOD

For when men are well [managed], they neither seek nor desire any other liberty. (*D*: 328)

MANAGEMENT INTEREST

The excesses of the people are directed against those whom they suspect of interfering with the public good; [while] those of princes are against apprehended interference with their individual interest. (*D*: 219)

MANAGEMENT RESPONSIBILITY

[W]hen the Senate and the people of Rome had resolved upon a war, . . . all the details of the campaign were left to the discretion and authority of the Consul, who could bring on a battle or not, and lay siege to this or that place, as seemed to him proper. . . . [F]or if they had required the Consul to conduct the war under orders from them, so to say, from hand to hand, it would have made [him] less circumspect, and more slow in his operations. . . . Besides this, the Senate would have undertaken to advise upon a matter which they could not have understood; for although there were many of the Senators who had great experience in war, yet not being on the spot, and not knowing the endless particulars which it is necessary to know to counsel wisely, they would have been liable to commit the most serious errors in attempting to instruct the Consul. And therefore they were willing that he should act entirely upon his own responsibility, and that he should reap all the glory, the love of which, they judged, would be his best check and rule of conduct. (*D*: 318)

MANAGEMENT BY TYRANNY

[T]hose tyrants who have the masses for friends and the nobles for enemies are more secure in the possession of their power, because their despotism is sustained by a greater force than that of those who have the people for their enemies and the nobles for their friends. (*D*: 186)

MANAGERS

They who from a private station become Princes by mere good fortune, do so with little trouble, but have much trouble to maintain themselves. They meet with no hindrance on their way, being carried as it were on wings to their destination, but all their difficulties overtake them when they alight. (*P*: 39)

MANAGERS, NEW

For the actions of a new Prince are watched much more closely than those of an hereditary Prince; and when seen to be good are far more effectual than antiquity of blood in gaining men over and attaching them to his cause. (*P*: 179)

MANAGERS, REWARDING

[W]hen a people or a prince has sent a general on some important expedition where by his success he acquires great glory, the prince or people is in turn bound to reward him. But if instead of such reward they dishonor and wrong him , influenced . . . by [greed], then they are guilty of an inexcusable wrong, which will involve them in eternal infamy. (*D*: 159)

MERGER

But when a Prince acquires a new [organization], joined on like a limb to his old possessions, he must disarm its inhabitants, except such of them as have taken part with him while he was acquiring it; and even these, as time and occasion serve, he should seek to render soft and [timid]; and he must so manage matters that all the arms of the new [organization] shall be in the hands of his own soldiers who have served under him in his ancient dominions. (*P*: 155)

But it may well happen that a [organization] lacking strength and good counsel in its difficulties becomes subject after a while to some neighboring [organization] that is better organized than itself; and if such is not the case, then they will be apt to revolve indefinitely in the circle of revolutions. (*D*: 102)

MIDDLE COURSE

[T]he middle course . . . is [deadly] in the extreme, when the question to be decided affects the fate of men. (*D*: 290)

MIDDLE MANAGERS

[A] Prince must always live with the same people, but need not always live with the same nobles, being able to make and unmake these from day to day, and give and take away their authority at his pleasure. (*P*: 67–68)

[A]s regards the nobles. . . . Those who so bind themselves [to your fortunes], and are not grasping, should be loved and honored. (*P*: 68)

[A] commander, judging that he will not be able to escape the fangs of ingratitude, . . . must do one of two things: either he must leave the army immediately after victory, and place himself at the disposal of his prince, carefully avoiding all show of insolence or ambition, so that the prince, deprived of all grounds of fear or suspicion, may reward him or at least not wrong him; or if this does not suit him, then he must boldly adopt the other course, and act in all respects as though he believed the conquest were for his own account, and not for his prince— conciliating to himself the good will of his army and of the subjected people, form- ing friendships and alliances with the neighboring princes, occupying the strongholds with his own men, corrupting the chiefs of his army and making sure of such as he cannot corrupt—and in this [way] seek to punish this prince in advance for the ingratitude which he is likely to show him. (*D*: 162)

MORALE

And if it happens that the people have no confidence in any one, as sometimes will be the case when they have been deceived before by events or men, then it will inevitably lead to the ruin of the [organization]. (*D*: 204)

MOTIVATING

[A] capable and courageous Prince will always overcome these difficulties [associated with being attacked by another organization] . . . by holding out hopes to his subjects that the evil will not be of long continuance; . . . by exciting their fears of the enemy's cruelty; and . . . by dexterously silencing those who seem to him too forward in their complaints. (*P*: 75–76)

MOTIVATION

[M]en work either from necessity or choice, and . . . it has been observed that virtue has more sway where labor is the result of necessity rather than of choice. (*D*: 96)

In truth, there never was any remarkable lawgiver [among] any people who did not resort to divine authority, as otherwise his laws would not have been accepted by the people; for there are many good laws, the importance of which is known to the sagacious lawgiver, but the reasons for which are not sufficiently evident to enable him to persuade others to submit to them; and therefore do wise men, for the purpose of removing this difficulty, resort to divine authority. (*D*: 127)

[E]very captain should endeavor to invent such as will encourage his own troops and dishearten those of the enemy. (*D*: 367)

[A] skillful commander should avoid with the utmost care everything that can possibly tend to discourage his army. And as nothing is so likely to do this as a check in the beginning, a general should beware of small combats, and should not permit them unless he can engage in them with decided advantage and the certain hope of victory. (*D*: 414)

MOTIVATION, APPROPRIATE TO THE SITUATION

When Soldiers are in their quarters, they are to be kept in order by fear and by punishment; when in the field, with hopes and rewards. (*A*: 520)

MOTIVATION OF EMPLOYEES

[So] that no sudden attack may be able to disorder your Soldiers, you must command them to stand ready with their arms, for things that are foreseen and expected, are less terrible and hurtful. (*A*: 494)

MOTIVES

Not only do princes pay no attention to pledges which they have been forced to give, when that force has ceased to exist, but they frequently disregard equally all other promises, when the motives that induced them no longer prevail. (*D*: 422)

NECESSITY

Prudent men make the best of circumstances in their actions, and, although constrained by necessity to a certain course, make it appear as if done from their own [generosity]. (*D*: 201)

A skillful general, then, w¹ ᴜ has to besiege a city, can judge of the difficulties of its capture by knowing and considering to what extent the inhabitants are under the necessity of defending themselves. If he finds that to be very urgent, then he may deem his task in proportion difficult; but if the motive for resistance is feeble, then he may count upon an easy victory. (*D*: 361)

NECESSITY, FIGHTING FROM

[Never fight with an Enemy reduced to despair.] When famine, natural necessity, or human passion has brought your Enemy to such despair, that impelled by that, he marches furiously to fight with you, you must keep within your Camp,and decline fighting as much as possibly you can. (*A*: 508)

NECESSITY, POWER OF

Equals in valor, you have the advantage of necessity, that last and most powerful of weapons! . . . [n]ecessity [is] the last and most powerful weapon. (*D*: 363)

NEW IDEAS

[There are] numerous instances of the important effect produced by some unforeseen incident caused by something new that is seen or heard in the midst of a conflict or heat of battle. (*D*: 366)

OBLIGATION

For it is the nature of men to incur obligation as much by the benefits they [give] as by those they receive. (*P*: 76)

[F]or no one will confess himself under obligation to anyone merely because he has not been injured by him. (*D*: 138)

ONE AGAINST MANY

[T]he presumption of success should always be in favor of a single power contending against a combination, however superior in numbers and power. For independent of the infinity of circumstances of which an individual can take advantage better than a combination of many, the former will always have the opportunity . . . to create divisions between the latter, and thus to weaken any powerful combination. (*D*: 359)

OPINIONS

During the period of the good Emperors he will see that golden age when everyone could hold and defend whatever opinion he pleased. (*D*: 125)

OPPONENTS

The Romans saw that by the defeat of an enemy's army they conquered a kingdom in a day, [while] the siege of a city which is obstinately defended may consume many years. (*D*: 317)

OPPONENTS OF CHANGE

All those become [the enemies of change] who were benefited by the tyrannical abuses and fattened upon the treasures of the prince, and who, being now deprived of these advantages, cannot remain content, and are therefore driven to attempt to re-establish the tyranny, so as to recover their former authority and advantages. (*D*: 138)

OPPORTUNITY

But while it was their opportunities that made these men fortunate, it was their own merit that enabled them to recognize these opportunities and turn them to account, to the glory and great [happiness] of their country. (*P*: 34)

OPPOSING

For in truth there is no better nor easier mode in [organizations], and especially in such as are corrupt, for successfully opposing the ambition of any citizen, than to occupy in advance of him those ways by which he expects to attain the rank he aims at. (*D*: 202)

OPPOSING FACTIONS

We observe, from the example of the Roman Consuls in restoring harmony beween the patricians and plebeians of Ardea, the means for obtaining that object, which is none other than to kill the chiefs of the opposing factions. In fact, there are only three ways of accomplishing it; the one is to put the leaders to death, . . . or to banish them from the city, or to reconcile them to each other under a pledge not to offend again. Of these three ways, the last is the worst, being the least certain and effective; for it is impossible that, after dissensions that have caused so much bloodshed and other outrages, a forced peace should be enduring. The parties meeting each other daily face to face will with difficulty abstain from mutual insults, and in their daily inter-course fresh causes for quarrel will constantly occur. (*D*: 391-92)

OPPRESSION

[M]en, in attempting to avoid fear themselves, give others cause for fear; and the injuries which they ward off from themselves they inflict upon others, as though there were a necessity either to oppress or to be oppressed. (*D*: 192)

OPTIMISM

And it is the more difficult to recognize these evils at their origin, as it seems natural to men always to favor the beginning of things; and these favors are more readily accorded to such acts as seem to have some merit in them. (*D*: 167)

ORDER, NEED FOR

He who pursues an Enemy that is disordered, in disorder himself; shall lose the victory he had gained, and perhaps give it to the Enemy. (*A*: 519)

ORGANIZATION

They who come to the Princedom . . . by virtuous paths, acquire with difficul-ty, but keep with ease. The difficulties they have in acquiring arise mainly from the new laws and institutions they are forced to introduce in founding and securing their government. (*P*: 34)

[A]s the organization of anything cannot be made by the many, because the divergence of their opinions hinders them from agreeing as to what is best, yet, when once they do understand it, they will not readily agree to abandon it. (*D*: 121)

[A]n undisciplined multitude is useless in war; for the least unexpected noise or word will throw them into confusion, and make them take to flight. (*D*: 367)

ORGANIZATION, CONTINUING

The welfare . . . of a [organization] does not consist in having a prince who governs it wisely during his lifetime, but in having one who will give it such laws that it will maintain itself even after his death. (*D*: 128)

ORIGINAL PURPOSE

[N]othing is more necessary for an [organization] than to restore to it from time to time the power and reputation which it had in the beginning, and to strive to have either good laws or good men to bring about such a result, without the necessity of the intervention of any [outside] force. (*D*: 323)

OVERTHROW

And therefore those who know themselves to be weak avoid [attempting to overthrow a prince], for where men's lives and fortunes are at stake they are not all insane; and when they have cause for hating a prince, they content themselves with cursing and vilifying him, and wait until someone more powerful and of higher position than themselves shall avenge them. (*D*: 332)

PARTICIPATIVE MANAGEMENT

[I]f we compare the faults of a people with those of princes, as well as their respective good qualities, we shall find the people vastly superior in all that is good and glorious. And if princes show themselves superior in the making of laws and in the forming of civil institutions and new statutes and ordinances, the people are superior in maintaining those institutions, laws, and ordinances, which certainly places them on a par with those who established them. (*D*: 218)

PARTICULARS

[I]n general matters the people are apt to deceive themselves, but rarely in particulars. (*D*: 197)

PASSION

[Where the enthusiasm of an army] is properly disciplined, it employs its impetuosity at the right time and with moderation; and no difficulties can abate or disconcert it. For good order sustains the courage and reanimates that [eagerness] with the hope of victory, which will never fail if discipline be preserved. (*D*: 412)

PAYBACKS

Men are more ready to repay an injury than a benefit, because gratitude is a burden and revenge a pleasure. (*D*: 159)

PERCEPTION

For it rarely happens that the victor in a battle loses many of his men; he loses only those that are killed in the fight, and none by flight; and in the heat of the action, when men are contending hand to hand, few are actually killed, because such a combat lasts but a short time. But even if it were continued longer, and many of the victorious army were slain, the prestige which follows victory and the terror which it brings with it are such that it greatly outweighs the loss which the conqueror suffers by the death of his men. So that an army that attacks him in the belief that he has been weakened, would find itself greatly mistaken, unless it should be sufficiently powerful to be able to have contended with him at any time even before the victory. (*D*: 288)

PERFORMANCE APPRAISALS

No more useful and necessary authority can be given to those who are appointed as guardians of the liberty of [an organization] than the faculty of accusing the citizens to the people, or to any magistrate or council, for any attempt against public liberty. Such a system has two very marked advantages for [an organization]. The first is, that the apprehension of being accused prevents the citizens from attempting anything against the [organization], and should they nevertheless attempt it, they are immediately punished, without regard to persons. The other is, that it affords a way for those evil dispositions that arise in one way or another against some one citizen to vent themselves; and when these ferments cannot in some way exhaust themselves, their promoters are apt to resort to some extraordinary means, that may lead to the ruin of the [organization]. (*D*: 114)

PERSPECTIVE

For as King Ferdinand said, ''men often act like certain small birds of prey, who, prompted by their nature, pursue their victims so eagerly that they do not see the larger bird above them, ready to pounce down upon and kill them.'' (*D*: 187)

PERSUASION

If we consider now what is easy and what difficult to persuade a people to, we may make this distinction: either what you wish to persuade them to represents at first sight gain or loss, or it seems brave or cowardly. And if you propose to them anything that upon its face seems profitable and courageous, though there be really a loss concealed under it which may involve the ruin of the [organization], the multitude will ever be most easily persuaded to it. But if the measure proposed seems doubtful and likely to cause loss, then it will be difficult to persuade the people to it, even though the benefit and welfare of the [organization] were concealed under it. (*D*: 205)

PLANS, WHEN TO CHANGE THEM

If you find the Enemy has any knowledge of your designs, you must change them. (*A*: 520)

PLOTS

[F]or the individual [acting alone] runs no risk before the execution of his plot, for as no one possesses his secret, there is no danger of his purpose coming to the ears of the prince. Any individual, of whatever condition, may form such a plot, be he great or small, noble or plebeian, familiar or not familiar with the prince; for everyone is permitted on occasions to speak to the prince, and thus the opportunity of satisfying his vengeance. (*D*: 331)

The execution of . . . a plot may be interrupted by the least false alarm, or by some unforeseen accident at the moment of its execution. (*D*: 343)

PLOTS, RISK OF COMMUNICATING

There are two risks . . . in communicating a plot to any one individual: the first, lest he should denounce you voluntarily; the second, lest he should denounce you, being himself arrested on suspicion, or from some indications, and being convicted and forced to it by torture. (*D*: 338)

POLICIES

Nothing confers such honor on a new ruler, as do the new laws and institutions he devises; for these when they stand on a solid basis and have a greatness in their scope, make him admired and venerated. (*P*: 194)

[P]overty and hunger make men industrious, and that the law makes men good; and if fortunate circumstances cause good to be done without constraint, the law may be dispensed with. But when such happy influence is lacking, then the law immediately becomes necessary. (*D*: 104)

For as good habits of the people require good laws to support them, so laws, to be observed, need good habits on the part of the people. (*D*: 143)

[N]o [organization] will ever be perfect if she has not by law provided for everything, having a remedy for every emergency, and fixed rules for applying it. (*D*: 171)

[I]ndividual men, and especially princes, may be charged with the same defects of which writers accuse the people; for whoever is not controlled by laws will commit the same errors as an unbridled multitude. (*D*: 215)

[O]ne should never allow an evil to run on out of respect for the law, especially when the law itself might easily be destroyed by the evil; and he should have borne in mind, that as his acts and motives would have to be judged by the result, in case he had been fortunate enough to succeed and live, everybody would have attested that what he had done was for the good of his country, and not for the advancement of any ambitious purposes of his own. (*D*: 326)

[I]n a well ordered army no one should do anything except in accordance with regulations. (*D*: 412)

POLICIES, OBSERVING

[T]here can be no worse example in a [organization] than to make a law and not to observe it; the more so when it is disregarded by the very parties who made it. (*D*: 190)

POLICIES, RETROSPECTIVE

[T]o attempt to eradicate an abuse that has grown up in a [organization] by the enactment of retrospective laws, is a most inconsiderate proceeding, and . . . only serves to accelerate the fatal results which the abuse tends to bring about; but by temporizing, the end will either be delayed, or the evil will exhaust itself before it attains that end. (*D*: 177)

POSITION

[O]n the side of the conspirator there are distrust, jealousy, and dread of punishment to deter him, while on the side of the Prince there are the laws, the majesty of the throne, the protection of friends and of the government to defend him. (*P*: 134–35)

POSITION, DEFENDING A DIFFICULT

The same fault is almost always committed by those who, upon the approach of an enemy, attempt to hold the difficult approaches, and to guard the passes; which course will almost always prove dangerous, unless you can conveniently place all your forces there, in which case that course may be adopted; but if the locality be so rugged that you cannot keep and deploy all your forces there, then it is dangerous. (*D*: 151)

POWER

[P]eople cannot make themselves secure except by being powerful. (*D*: 97)

[F]or Power can easily take a name [a title], but a name cannot give power. (*D*: 169)

For when full power is conferred for any length of time (and I call a year or more a long time) it is always dangerous, and will be productive of good or ill effects, according to [whether] those upon whom it is conferred are themselves good or bad. (*D*: 172)

[T]hat which generally produces ruptures between great powers . . . is sometimes due to accident, or it results from the policy of the party that desires to make the war. (*D*: 249)

POWER ALIGNMENTS

True, some people say that one should not keep so close to princes as to be involved in their ruin, nor so far away but what in case of their ruin you might thereby advance your own fortunes. This middle course would undoubtedly be the best to pursue, but as I believe that impossible, [you must] either . . . go away from them entirely, or . . . attach yourself very closely to them; and whoever attempts any other way, even though he be a personage of distinction, exposes himself to constant danger. (*D*: 324)

POWER, DESIRE FOR

[T]his desire to reign is so powerful that it not only dominates the minds of those born with the expectation of a throne, but also that of those who have no such expectations. (*D*: 327)

PRAISING THE PAST

Men ever praise the olden time, and find fault with the present, though often without reason . . . [t]he reasons which cause this illusion are various. The first . . . to be the fact that we never know the whole truth about the past, and very frequently writers conceal such events as would reflect disgrace upon their century, [while] they magnify and amplify those that lend lustre to it. . . . Another reason is that men's hatreds generally spring from fear or envy. Now, these two powerful reasons of hatred do not exist for us with regard to the past, which can no longer inspire either apprehension or envy. But it is very different with the affairs of the present, in which we ourselves are either actors or spectators, and of which we have a complete knowledge, nothing being concealed from us; and knowing the good together with many other things that are displeasing to us, we are forced to conclude that the present is inferior to the past, though in reality it may be much more worthy of glory and fame. (*D*: 223)

PREDICTING

Whoever considers the past and the present will readily observe that all cities and all peoples are and ever have been animated by the same desires and the same passions; so that it is easy, by diligent study of the past, to foresee what is likely to happen in the future in any [organization], and to apply those remedies that were used by the ancients, or, not finding any that were employed by them, to devise new ones from the similarity of the events. (*D*: 180)

PREPARATION

For a general who disposes his army in such manner that it can rally three . . . times in the course of a battle, must have fortune against him three times before being defeated, and must have an enemy opposed to him sufficiently superior to overcome him three times. But if an army can resist only a single shock, . . .

it may easily lose the battle; for with the slightest disorder even the most mediocre courage may carry off the victory. (*D*: 266)

The Rich Man unarmed, is but a prey to the Soldier. (*A*: 520)

PRESTIGE

Want of firmness in the execution [of a plot against a prince] arises either from respect, or from innate cowardice of him who is to commit the act. Such is the majesty and reverence that ordinarily surrounds the person of a prince, that it may easily mitigate the fury of a murderer, or fill him with fear. (*D*: 340–41)

PRETENDING

[Y]et if we well consider his conduct [in pretending to be a fool] we are led to believe that he had another reason, which was that by thus avoiding observation he would have a better chance of destroying the kings, and of liberating his country, whenever an opportunity should offer. (*D*: 324)

PRINCIPLES

This return of a [organization] to its original principles is either the result of [external] accident or of [internal] prudence. (*D*: 319)

PRIVILEGES

And though all your subjects cannot be armed, yet if those of them whom you arm be treated with marked favor, you can deal more securely with the rest. For the difference which those whom you furnish with arms perceive in their treatment, will bind them to you, while the others will excuse you, recognizing that those who incur greater risk and responsibility merit greater rewards. (*P*: 154)

PROBLEMS

[I]n all human affairs . . . you cannot avoid one inconvenience without incurring another. (*D*: 112)

PROBLEM SOLVING

For when you are on the spot, disorders are detected in their beginnings and remedies can be readily applied; but when you are at a distance they are not heard of until they have gathered strength and the case is past cure. . . . In short, where the Prince resided in person, it will be most difficult to oust him. (*P*: 8–9)

([W]hen any evil arises within an [organization], or threatens it from without, that is to say, from an intrinsic or extrinsic cause, and has become so great as to fill everyone with apprehension, the more certain remedy by far is to temporize with it, rather than to attempt to extirpate it; for almost invariably he who attempts to crush it will rather increase its force, and will accelerate the harm apprehended from it. (*D*: 167)

PROCEDURES

Now, there is no more effectual way for putting an end to calumnies than to introduce the system of legal accusations, which will be as beneficial to [organizations] as [slanders] are injurious. (*D*: 118)

PROFIT SHARING

[F]or when a Town was taken, or an Army defeated, all the prize was brought into a public place, and distributed man by man; according to everyone's merit. (*A*: 492)

PROJECT MANAGERS

[T]here is no easier way to ruin [an organization] where the people have power, than to involve them in daring enterprises, for where the people have influence they will always be ready to engage in them, and no contrary opinion will prevent them. But if such enterprises cause the ruin of [organizations], they still more frequently cause the ruin of the particular citizens who are placed at the head to conduct them. (*D*: 206–7)

PROMISES EXACTED BY FORCE

[T]here is no disgrace in disregarding promises that have been exacted by force. Promises touching public affairs, and which have been given under the pressure of force, will always be disregarded when that force no longer exists, and this involves no dishonor. (*D*: 422)

PRUDENCE

Failure in the execution [of a plot] result from lack of prudence or courage; men are seized by one or the other of these feelings, which confuse their brains and make them say and do things that they ought not. (*D*: 341)

PUNISHMENT

For if [the generals'] misconduct was intentional, they punished them humanely; and if it was caused by ignorance, they not only did not punish them, but rewarded and honored them nevertheless, . . . for they judged that it was of the greatest importance for those who commanded their armies to have their minds entirely free and unembarrassed by any anxiety other than how best to perform their duty, and therefore they did not wish to add fresh difficulties and dangers to a task in itself so difficult and perilous, being convinced that, if this were done, it would prevent any general from operating vigorously. (*D*: 163–64)

[O]ne of the most important points to be considered by him who wishes to establish a [organization] is the question in whose hands he shall place the power over the life and death of its citizens. (*D*: 199)

For the love of country had more power over them than any other sentiment; and they thought so much more of its present dangers, to which the ambition of Manlius exposed them, than of his past services, that they saw no other way of relieving themselves of those dangers than by his death. (*D*: 352)

QUALITY CIRCLES

[I]t is the nature of the multitude either humbly to serve or insolently to dominate. (*D*: 215)

QUESTIONS

[F]or a wise question makes a man consider many things which perhaps he regarded not before; and understand others, which without interrogation he had never understood. (*A*: 436)

RECOMMENDATIONS, MAKING

[The] dangers to which those expose themselves who counsel [an organization] or a prince to undertake some grave and important enterprise in such a manner as to take upon themselves all the responsibility of the same. For as men only judge of matters by the result, all the blame of failure is charged upon him who first advised it; [while] in case of success he receives commendations, but the reward never equals the punishment. (*D*: 409)

RELYING ON OTHERS

[A] Prince, therefore, must not build on what he sees in tranquil times when the [employees] feel the need of the [organization]. For then everyone is ready to run to promise, and, danger of death being remote, even to die for the [organization]. But in troubled times, when the [organization] has need of its [employees], few are to be found. And the risk of the experiment is the greater in that it can only be made once. (*P*: 72)

REORGANIZATION

Those thus injured [who have been deprived of their fields and houses to bestow them on the new inhabitants] form but a small part of the community, and remaining scattered and poor can never become dangerous. All others being left unmolested, are in consequence easily quieted, and at the same time are afraid to make a false move, lest they share the fate of those who have been deprived of their possessions. (*P*: 9–10)

But losing the head [while] the trunk was still sound, it was easy to restore Rome to liberty and proper institutions. And it must be assumed as a well-demonstrated truth, that a corrupt people that lives under the government of a prince can never become free, even though the prince and his whole line should be destroyed by another. For a people in such condition can never become settled unless a new prince be created, who by his good qualities and valor can maintain their liberty. (*D*: 141)

Whoever becomes prince of a [organization] especially if the foundation of his power is feeble, . . . will find the best means for holding that [organization is] to [structure] the government entirely anew (he himself a new prince there); . . . he should leave nothing unchanged in that province, so that there should be neither rank, nor grade, nor honor, nor wealth, that should not be recognized as coming from him. (*D*: 155–56)

[W]here the body of the people is so thoroughly corrupt that the laws are powerless for restraint, it becomes necessary to establish some superior power which, with a royal hand, and with full and absolute powers, may put a curb upon the excessive ambition and corruption of the powerful. (*D*: 210–11)

[A]nyone charged with the defense of a city should avoid, as a dangerous rock, the arming of a tumultuous multitude; but he should select and enroll those whom he wants to arm, and teach them whom they have to obey, the places for assembling, and where to march; and then he must order those who are not enrolled to remain at home to protect their houses. (*D*: 399)

REPUTATION

[N]othing is so infirm and fleeting as a reputation for power not founded upon inherent strength. (*P*: 102)

[A] wise Prince, when he has the occasion, ought dexterously to promote hostility to himself in certain quarters, in order that his greatness may be enhanced by crushing it. (*P*: 157)

Nothing makes a Prince so well thought of as to undertake great enterprises and give striking proofs of his capacity. (*P*: 163)

Sometimes [organizations] are built by a prince, not for the purpose of living there, but merely as monuments to his glory; . . . but as all these [organizations] are at their very origin deprived of liberty, they rarely succeed in making great progress, or in being counted [among] the great powers. (*D*: 96)

For there is no better indication of a man's character than the company which he keeps; and therefore very properly a man who keeps respectable company acquires a good name, for it is impossible that there should not be some similitude of character and habits between him and his associates. Or . . . a man acquires this good reputation by some extraordinary act, which, although relating to private matters, will still obtain him celebrity if it be honorably performed. [Of the two] the last is the most influential. (*D*: 406–7)

RESERVES, NEED FOR

It is better in the drawing up your Battalions for a Battle, to draw them up with reserves, and place such behind the front as may supply it upon occasion; than to enlarge your front, and make as it were but one rank of your whole Army. (*A*: 519)

RESOURCES

Men, Arms, Money and Provisions are the nerves of War; but the first two are most necessary, because Men and Arms will find Money and [provisions], but Money and [provisions] can never find Men. (*A*: 520)

And money alone, . . . far from being a means of defense, will only render a prince the more liable to being plundered. There cannot, therefore, be a more erroneous opinion than that money is the sinews of war. . . . I maintain, then, contrary to the general opinion, that the sinews of war are not gold, but good soldiers; for gold alone will not procure good soldiers, but good soldiers will always procure gold. . . . But by making their wars with iron, they [the Romans] never suffered for the want of gold; for it was brought to them, even into their camp, by those who feared them. (*D*: 252)

He who makes not provisions for [supplies and resources], will be beaten without a blow. (*A*: 519)

RESPONSIBILITY

[Whom should be trusted to maintain an open organization—the managers or the managed?] [If the desire is to expand your empire,] . . . one should always confide any [right] to those who have least desire of violating it; and doubtless, if we consider the object of the nobles and of the people, we must see that the first have a great desire to dominate, [while] the latter have only the wish not to be dominated, and consequently a greater desire to live in the enjoyment of liberty; so that when people are intrusted with the care of any privilege or liberty, being less disposed to encroach upon it, they will of necessity take better care of it; and being unable to take it away themselves, will prevent others from doing so. . . . [However, if the desire is only to maintain your empire] the preference given to the nobility, as guardians of public liberty, has two advantages: the first, to yield something to the ambition of those who, being more engaged in the management of public affairs, find, so to say, in the weapon which the office places in their hands, a means of power that satisfies them; the other, to deprive the restless spirit of the masses of an authority calculated from its very nature to produce trouble and dissensions, and apt to drive the nobles to some act of desperation, which in time may cause the greatest misfortunes. (*D*: 107–8)

[I]n a well-ordered [organization] a man's merits should never [blot out] his crimes. (*D*: 150)

Now, the commander of [a great] expedition would naturally feel the weight of all the cares attendant on such enterprises, and which are very great. But if in addition to these anxieties the mind of the general had been disturbed by the examples of other generals who had been crucified, or otherwise put to death, for having lost battles, it would have been impossible for him, under the influence of such apprehensions, to have proceeded vigorously. Judging, therefore, that the ignominy of defeat would be sufficient punishment for such a commander, they did not wish to terrify him with other penalties. (*D*: 164)

RESTRAINTS

[Because people are easily corrupted and become wicked and can be influenced to do wrong by powerful people, organizations] will [be] prompt in restraining the passions of men, and depriving them of all hopes of being able to do wrong with impunity. (*D*: 188)

RESTRUCTURING

And as the [restructuring of an organization] presupposes a good man, [while] the making of himself prince of [an organization] by violence naturally presupposes a bad one, it will consequently be exceedingly rare that a good man should be found willing to employ wicked means to become prince even though his final object be good; or that a bad man, after having become prince should be willing to labor for good ends, and that it should enter his mind to use for good purposes that authority which he has acquired by evil means. (*D*: 145)

RESULTS

[I]n the actions of all men, and most of all the Princes, where there is no tribunal [to appeal to], we look to results. Wherefore if a Prince succeeds in establishing and maintaining his authority the means will always be judged honorable and be approved by everyone. (*P*: 129–30)

[A]ll evil examples have their origin in good beginnings. (*D*: 192)

REVENGE

[A]ll rulers [should] remember never to esteem a man so lightly as to believe that, having heaped injuries and insults upon him, he will not seek to revenge himself, even at the risk of his own life. (*D*: 307)

A prince . . . should be most careful to avoid touching [a person's benefits] for he can never despoil a man so completely but what he will cherish a determined desire for revenge. (*D*: 330)

REWARDS

But to preserve a wholesome fear of punishment for evil deeds, it is necessary not to omit rewarding good ones. (*D*: 153)

RISK

[You] should never risk [your] whole fortune with only a portion of [your effort]. (*D*: 150)

ROCK AND A HARD PLACE, BETWEEN A

Of all the unhappy conditions to which princes or [organizations] can be reduced, the most unhappy is that when they are unwilling to accept peace and incapable of sustaining war; and to this condition those are reduced who consider themselves oppressed by the terms of peace, and who, if they wished to make war, would have to yield themselves a prey to their allies, or victims to their enemies. (*D*: 289)

ROOKIES

[I]f great commanders have employed extraordinary means for reassuring veteran troops, much greater precautions are necessary with fresh troops that have never before met an enemy face to face. For if an unaccustomed enemy can inspire veteran troops with terror, that feeling must be infinitely greater with raw troops, who for the first time encounter an enemy of any kind. (*D*: 417)

RUMORS

Accusations must be brought before the magistrates, or the people, or the councils, [while slanders and rumors] are spread in public places as well as in private dwellings; and [these] are more practiced where the system of accusations does not exist, and in [organizations in which policy] does not admit to them. (*D*: 118)

SALARIES, NEED TO PAY WELL

The chief thing incumbent upon a General is to pay well, and punish well; . . . for you cannot in justice chastise any [misdeeds] in a Soldier, when you disappoint him of his pay. (*A*: 507)

SECRETS

For either the secret communications are discovered before the execution of the plan, which happens very easily, either by the treachery of those to whom the secret has been communicated, or by difficulties in the execution, having to deal with enemies with whom it is not permitted to hold any communication. (*D*: 316)

[T]he most prudent course is not to communicate the plot to any one, . . . and if you cannot avoid drawing someone into your confidence, then to let it be not more than one, for in that case the danger is much less than if you confide in many. (*D*: 338)

No resolution is so likely to succeed, as that which is concealed from the Enemy till it comes to be executed. (*A*: 519)

SELF-APPRAISAL

[P]rinces or magistrates who wish to destroy [evils in their organizations] must watch all points, and must be careful in attacking them not to increase instead of diminishing them, for they must not believe that a fire can be extinguished by blowing upon it. They should carefully examine the extent and force of the evil, and if they think themselves sufficiently strong to combat it then they should attack it regardless of consequences; otherwise they should let it be, and in no wise attempt it. (*D*: 168)

SERVICE

For although the Romans were great lovers of glory, yet they did not esteem it dishonorable to obey those whom they had at a previous time commanded, or to serve in that army of which themselves had been chiefs. (*D*: 173)

SITUATION

The situation of the place is sometimes more effectual then the courage of your men. (*A*: 519)

SLACKING OFF

[W]hen Princes devote themselves rather to pleasure than to arms, they lose their dominions. (*P*: 103)

SPIES, NEED FOR

[When penetrating an enemy's organization you should] send out spies and guides with guards, promising them rewards if they tell [the truth], and threatening them with punishment [if they lie]. But above all [be careful] that [your] Army knows nothing of his design; for in the whole Art of War there is nothing so useful, as to conceal the enterprises that you are about. (*A*: 493)

STAFF RELATIONS

[A] Prince can never secure himself against a disaffected people, their number being too great, while he may against a disaffected nobility, since their number is small. (*P*: 67)

STRENGTH IN COURAGE

The courage of Soldiers is better than their number. (*A*: 519)

STRIFE

[Creating divisions within an organization] argues weakness in a Prince, for under a strong government such divisions would never be permitted, since they are profitable only in time of peace as an expedient whereby subjects may be more easily managed; but when war breaks out their futility is revealed. (*P*: 157)

SUCCESS

In important affairs it is necessary for success that the principal authority should reside in one man only. (*D*: 369)

SUCCESSORS

The lawgiver should . . . be sufficiently wise and virtuous not to leave . . . authority which he has assumed either to his heirs or to any one else; for mankind, being more prone to evil than to good, his successor might employ for evil purposes the power which he had used only for good ends. (*D*: 121)

[W]e may note that a successor of less vigor and ability than the first king may yet be able to maintain [an organization] established by the genius and courage of his predecessor, and may enjoy the fruits of his labors. But if it should happen that his life be a long one, or that his successor should not have the same good qualities and courage as the first king, then the government will necessarily go to ruin. (*D*: 146–47)

Two continuous successions of able and virtuous princes will achieve great results. (*D*: 148)

SURVIVAL

[W]here the very safety of the country depends upon the resolution to be taken, no considerations of justice or injustice, humanity or cruelty, nor of glory or of shame, should be allowed to prevail. But putting all other considerations aside, the only question should be, What course will save the life and liberty of the country? (*D*: 421)

TACTICS

[A] wise Prince should devise means whereby his subjects may at all times, whether favorable or adverse, feel the need of the [organization] and of him, for then they will always be faithful to him. (*P*: 72)

A good general . . . has to do two things; the one, to try by novel stratagems to create alarm amongst the enemy; and the other, to be on his guard to discover those that the enemy may attempt to practise upon him, and to render them fruitless. (*D*: 367)

[T]he commander of an army should always mistrust any manifest error which he sees the enemy commit, as it invariably conceals some stratagem. For it is not reasonable to suppose that men will be so incautious. But the desire for victory often blinds men to that degree that they see nothing but what seems favorable to their object. (*D*: 428–29)

TACTICS, VARYING

To overreach and circumvent an enemy, it is good sometimes to vary your custom that the Enemy depending upon it, may be disappointed and ruined. Thus it happened with a General, who being accustomed to give [a certain] signal of the approach of the Enemy [changed it] the Enemy supposing he was not perceived, (because he saw no signal given) marched on in disorder, and gave his Adversary the victory. (*A*: 508)

TACTICS, WHEN YOU ARE IN TROUBLE

[I]t would . . . contribute much to the freeing a man from the power of the Enemy, to do something . . . that may keep him in suspense. [First] by assaulting him with part of your forces, that while he is employed upon them, the rest may have time to preserve themselves. [Second] . . . by contriving some new thing or other that may amuse or astonish the Enemy, and render him uncertain [what he is to do.] (*A*: 506)

TAKEOVERS

He [who acquires an organization], if he means to keep it, must see to two things; first, that the blood of the ancient line of Princes be destroyed; second, that no change be made in respect of laws or taxes; for in this way the newly acquired [organization] speedily becomes incorporated with the [established organization]. (*P*: 7–8)

[W]hoever becomes master of a [organization] accustomed to live free and does not destroy it, may reckon on being destroyed by it. . . . [d]o what you will, and take what precautions you may, unless the inhabitants be scattered and dispersed, . . . the old order of things, will never cease to be remembered, but will at once be turned against you whenever misfortune overtakes you. (*P*: 29–30)

[Organizations] suddenly acquired, like all else that is produced and grows up rapidly, can never have such root or hold as that the first storm that strikes them shall not overthrow them; unless, indeed . . . they who thus suddenly become Princes have a capacity for learning quickly how to defend what Fortune has placed in their lap, and can lay those foundations after their rise [before they are destroyed]. (P: 40)

[Of reorganization and takeovers,] some are effected by bloodshed, and others without any. . . . This depends upon whether the [organization] that changes . . . does so by violence, or not. When effected by violence the change will naturally inflict suffering upon many; these in turn will desire to revenge themselves, and from this desire of revenge results the shedding of blood. But when such a change is effected by the general consent of [those], who have made the [organization] great, then there is no reason why the people should wish to harm any one but the chiefs of the [organization]. (D: 35)

[O]ther powers that are more distant [than an organization being taken over] and have no immediate intercourse with him, will look upon this as a matter too remote for them to be concerned about, and will continue in this error until the conflagration spreads to their door, when they will have no means for extinguishing it except their own forces, which will no longer suffice when the fire has once gained the upper hand. (D: 228)

[A]s all the actions of men resemble those of nature, it is neither natural nor possible that a slender trunk should support great branches; and thus a small [organization] cannot conquer and hold cities and kingdoms that are larger and more powerful than herself, and if she does conquer them, she will experience the same fate as a tree whose branches are larger than the trunk, which will not be able to support them, and will be bent by every little breeze that blows. (D: 236)

[A method for organizational growth is] to make the conquered people immediately subjects, and not associates. (D: 238)

And by . . . terminating each war promptly . . . [and] exhausting at the same time their enemies by the constant renewal of the wars, and by defeating their armies and devastating their territories, and imposing conditions that were most advantageous to themselves, the Romans steadily increased their wealth and power. (D: 245)

[I]t is impossible for a [organization] to remain long in the quiet enjoyment of her freedom within her limited confines; for even if she does not molest others, others will molest her, and from being thus molested will spring the desire and necessity of conquests, and even if she has no foreign foes, she will find domestic enemies [among] her own citizens, for such seems to be the inevitable fate of all large cities. (D: 279)

TAKEOVERS, HOSTILE

[After a hostile takeover] if instead of colonies you send troops, the cost is far greater, and the whole revenues of the [organization] are spent in guarding it; so that the gain becomes a loss, and much wider offense is given. (*P:* 10)

[O]n seizing [an organization], the usurper should [think] of all the injuries he must inflict, and inflict them all at a stroke, that he may not have to renew them daily, but be enabled by their discontinuance to reassure men's minds, and win them by benefits. (*P:* 63)

TAKEOVERS, METHOD

It is better to conquer an Enemy by hunger than fighting. (*A:* 519)

TAKEOVERS, SUDDEN AND SECRET

[A] Town is taken with more ease, when it is suddenly attacked, as when an Army keeps at such a distance, as that the Town believes either you will not at all, or cannot attempt it before they shall [sound] the alarm of your motion, because it is [so far off]. Wherefore if you can come upon them suddenly and secretly, [the great majority of the time] you will succeed in your design. (*A:* 515)

TAKING YOUR OWN MEDICINE

[T]he best remedy to be used against the design of an enemy, is to do that bravely of your self, to which you perceive he would endeavor to force you: for doing it voluntarily you do it orderly, and to your own profit and advantage; whereas if you do it by constraint, you do it to your ruin. (*A:* 482–83)

TAKING YOUR TIME

A prince therefore should be slow in undertaking any enterprise upon the representations of exiles, for he will generally gain nothing by it but shame and serious injury. (*D:* 314)

[It has often been thought wise that a general has] contented himself with merely sustaining the shock of the enemy, judging a slow and deliberate attack to be the most advantageous, and reserved the [eagerness] of his troops for the last, when the enemy's [enthusiasm] for combat and his fire had somewhat cooled down. (*D:* 426)

THREATS

[T]o threaten is more dangerous for princes, and more frequently causes conspiracies, than the actual injury itself; and therefore princes should guard against indulging in menaces. (*D:* 339)

TIME, BUYING

If a General be blocked up in his Camp by the Enemy, he cannot do better than to propose an accord, or at least a truce with him for some days, for that makes your Enemy the more negligent in everything; [in which] you may take your advantage, and give him the slip. (*A*: 505)

TIME SHOWS ALL THINGS

[W]hoever desires to found [an organization] and give it laws, must start with assuming that all men are bad and ever ready to display their vicious nature, whenever they may find occasion for it. If their evil disposition remains concealed for a time, it must be attributed to some unknown reason; and we must assume that it lacked occasion to show itself; but time, which has been said to be the father of all truth, does not fail to bring it to light. (*D*: 104)

TITLES

[I]t is not titles that honor men, but men [who] honor the titles. (*D*: 417)

TRAINING

For whoever wishes to form a good army must, by real or sham fights, train his troops to attack the enemy sword in hand, and to seize hold of him bodily. (*D*: 272)

[T]roops cannot be good unless they are well disciplined and trained, and this cannot be done with any troops other than natives of the country; for [an organization] is not and cannot be always engaged in war, therefore troops must be trained and disciplined in time of peace, and this can only be done with [your own employees], on account of the expense. (*D*: 402)

TRAINING, NEED FOR

He who in War is most vigilant to observe the designs and enterprises of the Enemy, and takes most pains in exercising and disciplining his Army, shall expose himself to less danger, and have greater probability of victory. (*A*: 519)

Your Soldiers despise things that are common, and are weary of anything that is tedious, I would advise therefore by [probing] and little skirmishes you acquaint your men with your Enemy before you bring them to Battle. (*A*: 519)

TREACHERY

If you suspect that there is anyone . . . that gives advice of your designs to the enemy; the best way to [take advantage] of his treachery, is, to [tell] some things to him which you never intend to do; and to conceal what you intend; to pretend doubts where you are perfectly resolved; and to conceal other things that you have absolutely determined; by [doing this] you will put the Enemy upon some enterprise (upon presumption that he knows your design) in which you may easily circumvent and defeat him. (*A*: 505)

If [organizations] are slower than princes, they are also less suspicious, and therefore less cautious; and if they show more respect to their great citizens, these in turn are thereby made more daring and audacious in conspiring against them. (*D*: 346)

TRICKS, BEWARE OF ENEMIES

[Don't be drawn in by the artifices of an enemy.] You must be cautious of believing anything easily, that is not reasonable to be supposed. . . . [If the enemy does something that looks too easy,] you must suspect there is some design at the bottom, and be careful it does not succeed. (*A*: 493)

TRICKS, DO NOT RELY ON ENEMIES

Those who are besieged, are to be very careful of the tricks and surprises of the Enemy, and therefore they are not to rely upon [the way he acts], but are rather to suspect there is some fraud or deceit that will fall heavily upon them, if they suffer themselves to be deluded. (*A*: 515)

TRUST

[An organization] should take great care not to intrust with an important administration one who has been gravely offended. (*D*: 372)

UNDERSTANDING WHAT IS GOING ON

He who understands his own Forces and his Enemies too, can hardly miscarry. (*A*: 519)

UNIONS

[F]or [while] on the one hand a loose mob without any leader is most formidable, yet on the other hand it is also most cowardly and feeble; and even if they are armed they will be easily subdued, if you can only shelter yourself against their first fury; for when their spirits are cooled down a little, and they see that they have all to return to their homes, they begin to mistrust themselves, and to think of their individual safety either by flight or submission. An excited multitude, therefore, that wishes to avoid such a result will have promptly to create a chief for itself, who shall direct and keep them united, and provide for their defense . . . (*D*: 214)

VICTORY

[A] general who has to choose between battle or flight will always prefer to fight, as then, even in the most doubtful case, there is still a chance of victory, [while] in flight his loss is certain anyhow. (*D*: 253)

Wise Princes and [organizations] should content themselves with victory; for when they aim at more, they generally lose. (*D*: 302)

[I]t is little things . . . that keep the soldiers united and confident, and these are essential elements of victory; though without courage they avail nothing. (*D*: 405)

VICTORY, PURSUE IT AFTER A BATTLE

[These are the things that happen after the Fight]. But since one of these two things must happen, either that we gain the Victory, or lose it; . . . when we gain it, we are to pursue it with the greatest diligence, and rather imitate Caesar in this [than] Hannibal, who for not following his Victory, and pushing it on after he had defeated the Romans . . . lost the whole Empire. . . . Caesar on the other [hand] never rested after a Victory, but followed the enemy with greater fury than he attacked them at first. (*A*: 482)

VIOLENCE

[T]o hold a government by violence, it is necessary that the oppressor should be more powerful than the oppressed. (*D*: 186)

WORKERS' GROUPS

[N]othing is more uncertain and inconstant than the multitude. (*D*: 214)

WRONGDOING, CORPORATE

[It is necessary to avoid doing wrong] either to an entire people or to an individual; for if any man be grievously wronged, either by an [organization] or by another individual, and satisfactory reparation be not made to him, if he lives in [an organization] he will revenge himself, even if it involves the ruin of the [organization], and if he lives under a prince, and be at all high-spirited, he will never rest until he has revenged himself upon him in some way, though he may see that it will cause his own ruin. (*D*: 306)

YIELDING

For it is almost always better to allow [anything] to be taken from [a prince] by force, rather than by the apprehension of force. For if he yields it from fear, it is for the purpose of avoiding war, and he will rarely escape from that. (*D*: 261)

YOUNG TURKS, OVERCOMING

[A General must be able to stop] mutinies and dissensions in his [organization]. The best way is by punishing the Ringleaders, but . . . it [must] be done so neatly, that they may have their reward before they have news [of what you intend to do]. The way to do that is, if they [are far away], to summon both guilty and innocent together. . . . [T]hinking themselves safe, and not in danger of any punishment, [they] may not be [obstinate], and stand up on their guard, but put themselves quietly into your hands to be Punished. If they be present, and at hand, the General is to make himself as strong as he can with those who are innocent, and others in whom he can confide, and then punish as he thinks fit. When the quarrel is private, and among themselves, the best way is to expose them to danger, and let them fight if they think good; for the fear of that does many times reconcile them. But above all things, there is nothing that keeps an Army so unanimous as the reputation of the General, which proceeds principally from his courage. (*A*: 507)

Appendix 2
The M Factor: Test Your Machiavellian IQ

What is your tendency to believe in or follow the principles of Machiavelli? This quiz gives you some indication of what I call the M Factor.

It is designed to measure your tendency toward "Machiavellian Traits." It does not measure goodness or badness—right or wrong. It is not a measurement of your total management style, but only a partial measurement of the type of manager you are. It should only be used as a relative measurement—not as a final forecast.

INSTRUCTIONS

Mark the statement that is most like you or that you agree with most with a plus (+) and the one that is least like you or that you agree with least with a minus (−).

There are no right or wrong answers. Do not select the answers that you think are the best; select the ones that best describe you.

After you have completed the questions, follow the instructions on how to score the inventory and then read the section on what your score means.

THE TEST

Item 1

A. It takes more imagination to be a successful criminal than a successful business person.

B. The phrase, "the road to hell is paved with good intentions" contains a lot of truth.

C. Most [people] forget more easily the death of a [parent] than the loss of their property.

Item 2

A. Men are more concerned about the car they drive than about the clothes their wives wear.

B. It is very important that imagination and creativity in children be cultivated.

C. People suffering from incurable diseases should have the choice of being put painlessly to death.

Item 3

A. Never tell anyone the real reason you did something unless it is useful to do so.

B. The well-being of the individual is the goal that should be worked on before anything else.

C. Since most people do not know what they want, it is only reasonable for ambitious people to talk them into doing things.

Item 4

A. People are getting so lazy and self-indulgent that it is bad for our country.

B. The best way to handle people is to tell them what they want to do.

C. It would be a good thing if people were kinder to others less fortunate than themselves.

Item 5

A. Most people are basically good and kind.

B. The best criteria for a wife or husband is compatibility—other characteristics are nice but not essential.

C. Only after a person has gotten what they want from life should they concern themselves with the injustices in the world.

Item 6

A. Most people who get ahead in the world lead clean, moral lives.

B. Any [man] worth his salt shouldn't be blamed for putting [his] career above [his] family.

C. People would be better off if they were concerned less with how to do things and more with what to do.

Item 7

A. A good teacher is one who points out unanswered questions rather than gives explicit answers.

B. When you ask someone to do something, it is best to give the real reasons for wanting it rather than giving reasons which might carry more weight.

C. A person's job is the best single guide as to the sort of person he is.

Item 8

A. The construction of such monumental works as the Egyptian pyramids was worth the enslavement of the workers who built them.

B. Once a way of handling problems has been worked out, it is best to stick to it.

C. One should take action only when sure it is morally right.

Item 9

A. The world would be a much better place to live in if people would let the future take care of itself and concern themselves only with enjoying the present.

B. It is wise to flatter important people.

C. Once a decision has been made, it is best to keep changing it as new circumstances arise.

Item 10

A. It is a good policy to act as if you are doing the things you do because you have no other choice.

B. The biggest difference between most criminals and other people is that criminals are stupid enough to get caught.

C. Even the most hardened and vicious criminal has a spark of decency somewhere within him.

Item 11

A. All in all, it is better to be humble and honest than to be important and dishonest.

B. A person who is able and willing to work hard has a good chance of succeeding in whatever they want to do.

C. If a thing does not help us in our daily lives, it isn't very important.

Item 12

A. A person shouldn't be punished for breaking a law that he thinks is unreasonable.

B. Too many criminals are not punished for their crimes.

C. There is no excuse for lying to someone else.

Item 13

A. Generally speaking, people won't work hard unless they are forced to do so.

B. Every person is entitled to a second chance, even after he commits a serious mistake.

C. People who can't make up their minds are not worth bothering about.

Item 14

A. A man's first responsibility is to his wife, not his mother.

B. Most men are brave.

C. It is best to pick friends that are intellectually stimulating rather than ones who are comfortable to be around.

Item 15

A. There are very few people in the world worth concerning oneself about.

B. It is hard to get ahead without cutting corners here and there.

C. A capable person motivated for his own gain is more useful to society than a well-meaning but ineffective one.

Item 16

A. It is best to give others the impression that you can change your mind easily.

B. It is a good working policy to keep on good terms with everyone.

C. Honesty is the best policy in all cases.

Item 17

A. It is possible to be good in all respects.

B. To help oneself is good; to help others even better.

C. War and threats of war are unchangeable facts of human life.

Item 18

A. P. T. Barnum was probably right when he said that there's at least one sucker born every minute.

B. Life is pretty dull unless one deliberately stirs up some excitement.

C. Most people would be better off if they controlled their emotions.

Item 19

A. Sensitivity to the feelings of others is worth more than poise in social situations.

B. The ideal society is one where everybody knows his place and accepts it.

C. It is safest to assume that all people have a vicious streak and that it will come out when they are given a chance.

Item 20

A. People who talk about abstract problems usually don't know what they are talking about.

B. Anyone who completely trusts anyone else is asking for trouble.

C. It is essential for the functioning of a democracy that everyone vote.

SCORING KEY

Score each item as follows: Each item should have one letter that has a plus (+) and one that has a minus (−) sign. For each item number find the selection that matches yours from the table. Look at the top of the column to see how many points that item is worth and enter the score next to the item number.

For example, on Item one. If you selected A as plus (+) and C as minus (−) you would score 1 point; if you selected B as plus and C as minus, or A as plus and B as minus, you would score 3 points; if you selected B as plus and A as minus, or C as plus and B as minus, you would score 5 points; if you selected C as plus and A as minus, you would score 7 points. Note that there are two possible selections for scores of 3 and 5 points. Add your scores for all the items. To this number add 20 points. This is your M-factor score.

WHAT YOUR SCORE MEANS

By itself the score has little meaning. The lowest possible score is 40 and the highest is 160. The higher the number, the more a person is apt to use Machiavellian tactics—or at least consider using them. Alternatively, the lower the score the less likely that person is to use Machiavellian tactics.

Beware of High Scorers

However, beware of those who score above 140. They are not Theory M managers, as discussed in this book, but more than likely are careless, caustic managers who are motivated by greed and gain. They should be considered extremely dangerous—avoid them when possible, beware of them when competing with them. They believe in winning power games at all costs and will sacrifice long-run peace of mind for short-term success. The danger is that in winning they will also sacrifice you. If you are in this category, you should consider changing your philosophy of management before it is too late.

The Theory M Manager

Theory M managers will usually score in a range from 100 to 140. However, depending on their situation and organizational position when taking the quiz they may score as low as 95.

While a score below 95 may indicate a weak manager, it may only indicate a stage of growth. Certainly, the lower the score the less the manager agrees with

Scoring Key for The M Factor
Points per Item

Item	1	3	5	7
1.	A+C-	B+C- A+B-	B+A- C+B-	C+A-
2.	A+C-	B+C- A+B-	B+A- C+B-	C+A-
3.	C+A-	B+A- C+B-	B+C- A+B-	A+C-
4.	A+B-	C+B- A+C-	C+A- B+C-	B+A-
5.	A+B-	C+B- A+C-	C+A- B+C-	B+A-
6.	A+C-	B+C- A+B-	B+A- C+B-	C+A-
7.	B+A-	B+C- B+C-	C+B- A+C-	A+B-
8.	C+B-	A+B- C+A-	A+C- B+A-	B+C-
9.	C+B-	A+B- C+A-	A+C- B+A-	B+C-
10.	A+B-	C+B- A+C-	C+A- B+C-	B+A-
11.	A+B-	C+B- A+C-	C+A- B+C-	B+A-
12.	C+B-	A+B- C+A-	A+C- B+A-	B+C-
13.	C+A-	B+A- C+B-	B+C- A+B-	A+C-
14.	B+C-	A+B- B+A-	A+B- C+A-	C+B-
15.	C+B-	A+B- C+A-	A+C- B+A-	B+C-
16.	C+B-	A+B- C+A-	A+C- B+A-	B+C-
17.	A+C-	B+C- A+B-	B+A- C+B-	C+A-
18.	C+A-	B+A- C+B-	B+C- A+B-	A+C-
19.	B+C-	A+C- B+A-	A+B- C+A-	C+B-
20.	A+B-	C+B- A+C-	C+A- B+C-	B+A-

Theory M principles, and in some cases he or she will actually be opposed to them. Scores of less than 60 probably indicate opposition. Even with a Theory M orientation, while they are learning both the art and science of management, new managers may have scores in this area. However, as they gain experience and become more effective, their scores will change. Experienced managers scoring in this area who feel the need to change need to learn to appreciate and adopt the principles outlined in this book and to modify portions of their philosophy of management.

While low scores—below 95—do not imply the dangers, at the individual level, that high scores do, they probably indicate an inability to be effective in management over the long run. Or at least they imply that the person will not be as effective as a person scoring higher, all other things being equal. Low scorers will not attack you very often, or if they do and you are prepared, they will fail.

At the organizational level, having an overabundance of these managers without an offsetting complement of effective Theory M managers might prove dangerous in a highly competitive environment. Certainly the nation with an inadequate supply of Theory M managers will lose its economic wars. So if you are selecting managers for your organization, use an individual's Theory M beliefs as one of the selection criteria.

Comparative Scoring

The results will be most useful to you as an individual if you compare your scores over a period of time. When doing this it is necessary to clear your mind (as much as possible) of your previous answers. Score each item as it applies to you at the time you are taking the test. Study the way your scores change in relation to things you are doing—increasing your education, thinking more about management, becoming more involved—to change your management methods.

Another way to use the test is to take it the way you think one of your opponents would answer the questions. Obviously the better you know your opponent the better you will be at judging his possible answers. From comparing and contrasting this person's actions with the score you computed for him, you should be able to get a "fix" on the accuracy of your selections. Once you have determined your opponent's "score," you should be able to predict how he will react to a given situation or to the tactics you are going to use in competition with him in organizational situations.

If you have the opportunity you can give the "questions" to your allies, opponents, and staff (without telling them why) in order to learn more about them. One way of accomplishing this is not to ask all the questions at once but just squeeze a question or two at a time into your normal conversations with them. Their scores, along with other information you have about them, may prove useful to you in dealing with them. Evaluating the results you receive from testing your staff should enable you to determine how they will respond in certain situations.

Remember, you should only use this information as a part of your analysis of yourself and others. Do not rely on it to answer all your questions. Use all your managerial insight in making judgments about yourself and others.

Selected Bibliography

Berle, A. A. *Power*. New York: Harcourt, Brace & World, 1969.

Bower, Joseph L. *The Two Faces of Management*. Boston: Houghton Mifflin, 1983.

Byrne, John A., Wendy Zellner, and Scott Ticer. "Caught in the Middle: Six Managers Speak Out on Corporate Life." *Business Week*, September 12, 1988, pp. 50–58.

Christie, R., and F. L. Geis. *Studies in Machiavellianism*. New York and London: Academic Press, 1970.

Copleston, Frederick. *A History of Philosophy*. Vol. 1, *Greece and Rome*. London: Search Press, 1946.

Cyert, R. M., and J. G. March. *A Behavioral Theory of the Firm*. Englewood Cliffs, N.J.: Prentice Hall, 1963.

Drucker, Peter. *The Practice of Management*. New York: Harper & Row, 1954.

Engels, Frederick. *Germany: Revolution and Counter Revolution*. New York: International Publishers, The Garden City, Press Limited, 1933.

Gulick, Luther, and Lynda Urwick. "Papers in the Science of Administration." New York: Institute of Public Administration, 1937.

Heilbroner, Robert L. *The Worldly Philosophers*. 5th ed., New York: Simon & Schuster, 1980.

Hittle, J. D. *The Military Staff: Its History and Development*. Harrisburg, Pa: Stackpole, 1961.

Katz, D., and R. L. Kahn. *The Social Psychology of Organizations*. New York: Wiley, 1966.

King, Preston. *The Ideology of Order: A Comparative Analysis of Jean Bodin and Thomas Hobbes*. London: Allen and Unwin, 1974.

Kolb, David A. *Organizational Psychology: A Book of Readings*. 3rd ed., Englewood, Cliffs, N.J.: Prentice-Hall, 1979.

Koontz, Harold, Cyril O'Donnell, and Heinz Weihrich. *Management*. New York: McGraw-Hill, 1984.

Machiavelli, Niccoló. *The Art of War in Seven Books*. Translated by Henry Neville. Printed for John Starkey, Charles Harper, and John Amery, London, 1680.

——— . *Discourses on the First Ten Books of Titus Livius*, from *The Historical, Political, and Diplomatic Writings of Niccoló Machiavelli, Volume II*. Translated from the Italian by Christian E. Detmold. Houghton, Mifflin and Company: Boston and New York, 1891.

——— . *The Prince*. Translated by Ninian Hill Thompson. Oxford: Clarendon, 1913.

Mansfield, Harvey C., Jr. *Taming the Prince*. New York: Free Press, 1989.

McClelland, D. C. "The Two Faces of Power." *Journal of International Affairs*, 1970, pp. 29–47.

McFillen, J. M. "Supervisory Power as Influence in Supervisor-Subordinate Relations," *Academy of Management Journal* 21 (1978): 419–33.

McGregor, D. *The Human Side of Enterprise*. New York: McGraw-Hill, 1960.

Meinecke, Friedrich. *The Doctrine of Raison d'État and Its Place in Modern History*. Translated by Douglas Scott. London: Routledge & Kegan Paul, 1984.

Mintzberg, Henry. *The Nature of Managerial Work*. Englewood Cliffs, N.J.: Prentice-Hall, 1980.

——— . *Power in and around Organizations*. Englewood Cliffs, N.J.: Prentice Hall, 1983.

Ouchi, William G. *Theory Z: How American Business Can Meet the Japanese Challenge*. Reading, Mass.: Addison-Wesley, 1981.

Plutarch. *Selected Lives and Essays*. Translated by Roper, Louis Loomis. New York: Rosyln, 1951.

——— . *The Rise and Fall of Athens*. Translated and Introduction by Kilvert, Ian Scott. New York: Penguin, 1960.

——— . *Fall of the Roman Empire*. Translated and Introduction by Seagar, Robin. New York: Penguin, 1972.

Pocock, J. G. A. *The Machiavellian Moment*. Princeton, N.J.: Princeton University Press, 1975.

Previte'-Orton, C. W. *The Shorter Cambridge Medieval History, Volume I: The Later Roman Empire to the Twelfth Century*. London: Cambridge University Press, 1971.

——— . *The Shorter Cambridge Medieval History, Volume II: The Twelfth Century to the Renaissance*. London: Cambridge University Press, 1971.

Robinson, Cyril E. *A History of the Roman Republic*. London: Methuen & Company Lt., 1966.

Schien, Edgar H. *Organizational Psychology, Third Edition*. Englewood Cliffs, N.J.: Prentice-Hall, 1980.

Sinnigen, William G., and Arthur E. R. Boak. *A History of Rome to AD 565, Sixth Edition*. New York: Macmillan Publishing Co., 1966.

Stogdill, R. M., and A. E. Coons. "Leader Behavior: Its Description and Measurement." Columbus: The Ohio State University Bureau of Business Research, 1957.

Tannenbaum, Robert, and Warren H. Schmidt. "How to Choose a Leadership Pattern," *Harvard Business Review*, May/June 1973, pp. 162–181.

Tocqueville, Alexis de. *Democracy in America*. Edited by J. B. Mayer, and Max Lerner. Translated by George Lawrence. New York: Harper & Row, 1966.

Vroom, Victor, and Phillip Yetton. *Leadership and Decision Making*. Pittsburgh: University of Pittsburgh Press, 1973.

Weber, Max. *The Theory of Social and Economic Organizations*. Edited by Talcott Parsons. Translated by Talcott Parsons and A. M. Henderson. New York: Oxford University Press, 1947.

——— . "The Essentials of Bureaucratic Organization: An Ideal-Type Construction." In *A Reader in Bureaucracy*. ed. Robert K. Merton et al., 18–27. New York: Free Press of Glencoe, 1952.

——— . "The Meaning of Discipline." In *From Max Weber: Essays in Sociology*, trans. and ed. H. H. Gerth and C. Wright Mills, 253. New York: Oxford University Press, 1958.

Weick, Karl E. *The Social Psychology of Organizing*. 2d ed. Menlo Park, Calif.: Addison-Wesley, 1979.

Winter, David G. *The Power Motive*. New York: Macmillan, 1973.

Index

Note that certain entries include codes in parentheses that refer to passages quoted from specific texts by Machiavelli.

About the Author

GERALD R. GRIFFIN is a management consultant specializing in individual and organizational behavior, training, information technology, and small business development. His most recent assignment took him to Botswana, Africa, as a U.S. Peace Corps volunteer, where he was Senior Lecturer/Consultant at the Institute of Development Management. While with IDM he performed consulting assignments within both the government and public sectors and taught management courses in Botswana, Swaziland, and Lesotho. He has been Vice President of Information Networking at Blue Cross and Blue Shield of Oklahoma and has taught administration of justice at Wichita State University.

His experiences include service as a U.S. Marine, as a Tulsa, Oklahoma, police officer, and as a U.S. Treasury agent. He is an advocate of the principle that business leaders should be involved in their communities and has devoted many hours to public service. He has written several journal articles, a series of Conflict in Management simulations, and a series of audio tapes on self-improvement. He earned a B.S. in Business Administration from The University of Tulsa, an M.B.A. from Southern Methodist University, and an Ed.D. from The University of Tulsa.